OFFERING HOSPITALITY

OFFERING
HOSPITALITY

Questioning Christian Approaches to War

CARON E. GENTRY

University of Notre Dame Press

Notre Dame, Indiana

Manufactured in the United States of America

Grateful acknowledgments to Suzanne Gardinier for permission
to quote excerpts from her poem "To Peace."

Library of Congress Cataloging-in-Publication Data
Gentry, Caron E.
    Offering hospitality : questioning Christian approaches to war / Caron E.
Gentry.
        pages   cm
    Includes bibliographical references and index.
    ISBN-13: 978-0-268-01048-5 (pbk.)
    ISBN-10: 0-268-01048-X (paper)
    1. War—Religious aspects—Christianity.   2. Pacifism—Religious aspects—
Christianity.   3. Agape.   4. Just war doctrine.   I. Title.
BT736.2.G39   2013
261.8'73—dc23

                        2013022546

To my students,

whose questions pushed me to write this book

and who have taught me so much

Contents

Acknowledgments

This book on hospitality was written due to the extension of hospitality. I am thankful for all of the sustenance that I received while writing it. In no certain order, I need to thank and acknowledge the following people and groups of people.

I will always be grateful to Abilene Christian University for providing me with my first academic position and for giving me the required space to write, especially to my provost, Jeanine Varner. The Cullen Grant committee was gracious enough to fund writing time for the summers of 2009 and 2010. Without both of these commitments, the book's schedule would have seriously lagged. My department was always hospitable to me and conscious of my need to write. Thank you especially to David and Mel.

In the fall of 2008, I enrolled part time in the Graduate School of Theology at ACU. This was a fateful decision that resulted in immense insight into the ideas presented here. Already a valued colleague, Fred Aquino became my professor, mentor, and friend. Thank you, Fred, for hours of conversation. Through my time in the GST, I also found some great friends and great readers—Lisa Sherman Nikolaus, Ryan Nikolaus, Wilson McCoy, Will Smith, Nic and Brittany Acosta.

My alma mater, the University of St. Andrews, welcomed me back to my intellectual home for a summer fellowship in 2009 and has since welcomed me back as a lecturer in the School of International Relations. The brief and lovely month of the fellowship helped me work through some of the more abstract and harder to grasp notions that are foundational to hospitality. Nick Rengger has always been one of my champions, and I want to thank him for specifically championing this project. Additional conversations with Tony Lang, Torsten Michel, Gurchathen Sanghera, and John Anderson helped me hone and further my thoughts. Since I have moved back to St. Andrews, these conversations have continued and further sustained by Jill Anderson, Karin Fierke, Jaremey McMullin, Jeffrey Murer, and Fiona McCallum.

International Studies Association-West has been another intellectual home for me. My previous coauthor, mentor, and friend, Laura Sjoberg, got me involved at ISA-West, and such involvement opened up a new world of intellectual friendships. The relationships I formed there have gifted me with insightful feedback; I'd like to thank Amy Eckert, Lisa Burke, Robert Williams, and Kim Hudson for planting valuable ideas in my head.

I am dedicating this book to my students because it owes an intellectual debt to some of the questions they raised. I have learned from all of my students. Still, this book is specifically dedicated to the students of HCOR 120: Honors Seminar in the Social Sciences, fall 2007 and spring 2008—thank you for being the most gracious guinea pigs ever. And, to the first International Relations and Christianity class of the fall of 2008, you all pushed me with your questions, comments, and participation. Thank you. Additionally, the students I went to Uruguay with are owed a certain privilege for being the ones who walked past my apartment day after day while I sat at the kitchen table furiously typing away.

Finally, I could not have written this book without the support of my family and friends. My interest in hospitality can stem only from having watched my parents, Tom and Liz Gentry, serve the church. My hope is that through some miracle the world is a better place for my nieces, Ela Gentry and Ashlyn Gentry, and for my godchildren,

Samuel Prokopchuk and Ella Johnson. Alaina Bearden served as an excellent editor—but all mistakes are mine. Many, many thanks to my editors at Notre Dame: Stephen Little and Barbara Hanrahan. To the four reviewers, your comments have done what reviews should do: strengthen the project. Conversations begun years ago in St. Andrews with Kristen and Trygve Johnson led to this book. More conversations in Aberdeen helped me clarify who I was writing this book for: thank you, Christine and Michael. Shelly, Kristina, Cole, and Dawne, thank you for listening to me talk about the book, be distracted by it, and for taking me to see Paul/Scott at the Beehive when I just couldn't write anymore.

Introduction

A Christian Response to Power

Set during the Mexican Civil War, Graham Greene's *The Power and the Glory* (1940) follows the life of a whisky priest as he tries to save his life and protect the faithful. There is no doubt that the priest is a fallen man—he is an alcoholic; he has had affairs with women in his parish; he is filled with self-loathing. While intent on doing penance, there is one thing he refuses to regret: that he's fathered a child. Shot and injured by a socialist lieutenant who hates everything the Catholic Church stands for, the priest runs for a gloomy three days before returning to danger to perform his priestly duties. For his effort, he is killed. The whisky priest is a Christ figure. This is hinted at even before his death. While evading the lieutenant and trying to minister to his congregants, the priest seeks out his graceless daughter. She is the encapsulation of dirty humanity. Nonetheless, the priest tries to impart to her an important lesson in the midst of a horrid war.

> He went down on his knees and pulled her to him, while she giggled and struggled to be free: "I love you. I am your father and I love you. Try to understand that." He held her tightly by the wrist and suddenly she stayed still, looking up at him. He said, "I would give my life, that's nothing, my soul . . . my dear, my dear, try to

understand that you are—so important." That was the difference, he had always known, between his faith and theirs, the political leaders of the people who cared only for things like the state, the republic: this child was more important than the whole continent. He said, "You must take care of yourself because you are so—necessary. The president up in the capital goes guarded by men with guns—but my child, you have all the angels of heaven" (Greene, 2005: 79).

There are some people who do not like to acknowledge the allusions to Christ in this undisciplined priest. Yet to deny this in part denies the dual nature of Christ: that the Word became flesh (John 1:14) to settle our sin because humanity is so important. In the Trinity, there is the Father that cares for his Son and for his children—his creatures inhabiting his creation—all interceded for by the Spirit. Scholars of international relations, with the discipline's focus on the state—on republics and tyrannies alike—and on all the continents, tend to lose sight of the children, of humanity, and forget that they are so very necessary. Humans require care. Care is not something easily and readily done in international relations—nonetheless, it is an essential practice in a world increasingly divided between the privileged who inhabit stable powerful states and those who are in weak, conflicted states and, thus, at considerable risk. Finding ways to care, to practice hospitality by seeing to the needs of those on the margins, is the purpose of this study.

There are multiple occasions in the Bible that Christians are taught to care. One such an example occurs in Luke 9:10–17, the feeding of the five thousand. The story is multilayered, but Jesus commands the Disciples to perform hospitality; when they want to send the crowd away, Jesus says, "'You give them something to eat.'"[1] (Which is more of a command than a request.) Still they protest, but after more instruction, they do as Jesus tells them. After feeding the crowd, there are twelve baskets filled with enough food for the Disciples. This is a clear story of hospitality and God's provision, but it is more than that. The Disciples, who struggle to grasp what Jesus is trying to tell them, in the end act without self-interest (even their suggestion to send the crowd away was selfless, "'Send the crowd away so they can go to the surrounding villages and countryside and find food and lodging'"). Acting without self-interest reaps them rewards: they are fed, along with everyone else.

Comprehending that the daughter of a drunken Catholic priest is important, indeed more important than the protected president or the state, upends notions of what is of primary concern in international relations (IR). Yet protecting without interest the good and the bad of humanity and humans is to practice hospitality in international affairs. Acting without self-interest is contrary to status quo understandings of how security operates. Nonetheless, this book explores how hospitality can be better inserted into understandings of war, specifically failed state conflicts, and ultimately of peace. Is peace a naïve objective? A blessed reality? An unreachable transcendent ideal? Practicing hospitality should result in peace; a new approach to *jus ad bellum*'s last resort is one method for practicing hospitality and establishing a better peace. The achievement of peace is intimately connected to the way we—the audiences of this book—look at war.

"We" is meant to include anyone reading this book, but it specifically references Christians in the United States who hope to engage a civil conversation about how we think about war and participate in governments that fight wars. "We" may also include non-Christians interested in reading a book that is critical of the conventional wisdom that seems to exist regarding U.S. Christians' thoughts on war. At its most basic point, hospitality is the relationship between different actors—actors who may respect one another on the highest level or actors who may resent and resist everything about the other. Yet in hospitality we extend courtesy and an audience to the other—we treat one another with respect, recognizing each other's humanity and intrinsic value. This book, with its focus on hospitality, is also asking people from different perspectives—theologians, feminists, postmodern scholars, and international relations experts—to engage in conversation with one another. The conversation may not be easy and may not be natural, but it is very important in light of the challenges facing the world today.

Christians, specifically those within the United States, are caught in the trappings of party politics and issues, mistakenly thinking that views on women's healthcare and taxes are predetermined by faith, instead of deeply personal and nuanced topics. Since 9/11, but more than likely beginning with the Moral Majority and the Reagan Administration, Christian thinking on war in the United States has become highly militaristic (see Bacevich, 2005). It is often assumed that American Christians think monolithically about what a faithful response to war is. But again, there are different perspectives due to different denominations and personal thinking on war. War is a complex issue. Christianity is also complex—there are multiple Christianities (denominations, churches, communities) in the United States, and within those, beliefs vary from person to person, with agreement largely centered on the faith that Jesus Christ is the resurrected Son of God. Citizenship and patriotism are additional complications. When Christians make generalizations about how "we" are to think about war and then how non-Christians ascribe generalizations to the Christian community about how "they" think about war, it is easy to see how conversations become difficult. Recognizing that there is a multitude of traditions within the Christian faith, this book cannot speak to or for them all. Yet the aim is to re-engage the traditional American Christian response to power, conflict, and war. This book re-evaluates the predominant strands of American political theology—Christian realism, pacifism, and the Just War tradition—to ask if these are the capstones to each strand's conversation or if they are now a point of departure for a new way of Christian thinking about war.

To do so, the strongest traditional American Christian voices within each strand—Reinhold Niebuhr, Stanley Hauerwas, and Jean Bethke Elshtain—are deconstructed in order to uncover a way for Christians to think critically about war in order to end complicity with it. Ending complicity may be too strong of a sentiment, because as people living in what is still the most powerful state in the world, a state that has only just ended one of two large and expensive so-called traditional wars, as well as having its finger in the pie of other recent and ongoing conflicts (e.g., Colombia, Libya, Pakistan, Israel/Palestine), U.S. citizens cannot completely end complicity—at most they can be aware of it, critical of it (criticism does not preclude support), and move against it when necessary. Being critical of our complicity with hegemonic power can happen only when we are given the tools to be aware of it.

The idea for this book emerged from the discussions during "A Christian Response to the New American Century," a Lilly Summer Fellows Institute event I participated in at Rosemont College, Rosemont, Pennsylvania, in 2005. The institute was directed toward examining how neoconservatives in the United States had manipulated Christian identity, but it also addressed a general Christian response to power. Since 2005, conversations, readings, questions in lectures, student projects, movies, and books have kept me thinking about the question, What is a Christian's response to power? Or at least this Christian's?

During the institute another fellow, Reverend Nicole Duran, brought up an interesting interpretation of the Strongman story in Mark 3. She posited that this parable speaks to power but more importantly speaks to those complicit with power. In this chapter in Mark, Jesus is not so critical of empire as much as he is critical of those who are at ease with this use of power, specifically the Jewish leaders who collaborated with Rome and members of the Jewish community who collaborated with those leaders. This position will be expanded upon in chapter 1, but, recognizing that this interpretation may be controversial to some, it still raises an important point: What relationship should Christians have with power? Is it something to be used to our advantage or something that we should shun? There are multiple answers to these questions.

Christian realism in international relations teaches that power is the way the world works; if one wants to understand global politics, one has to understand power. There is some truth to this statement. Pacifism teaches that humans can neither understand nor claim power because true power is exemplified in the metaphysical awesomeness of God. There is some truth to this statement as well. There are those that argue that the Just War tradition might be where both Christian realism and pacifism end.[2] For instance, if Christian realists believe that the balance of power will prevent war (for as much as war may be inevitable, they do not want it), then once the balance of power fails and war does happen, the question becomes, How can we best fight war? The answer might be: justly. Some pacifists admit that war happens but hate it, and some pacifists sometimes see war as the very last option. But then the question remains, When it does happen (and it does) how can we best fight it? The answer might be: justly.

Yet, there are Christians who are also using Just War to argue in a way that strikes precariously close to American imperialism (Elshtain, 2004). The Just War tradition is not without its own critics; Nick Rengger has been quoted multiple times as saying, "Just War is after all just war." No matter how much Just War advocates try to make war more palatable by setting restrictions on the entering and fighting of it, it is still death and destruction. Yet, Just War may offer figurative space for a solution, where the expansion and weakening of traditional definitions of last resort create hospitality instead of war. In thinking through a response to power, this passage from Romans became foundational:

> Love must be sincere. Hate what is evil; cling to what is good. Be devoted to one another in brotherly love. Honor one another above yourselves. Never be lacking in zeal, but keep your spiritual fervor, serving the Lord. Be joyful in hope, patient in affliction, faithful in prayer. Share with God's people who are in need. Practice hospitality.
>
> Bless those who persecute you; bless and do not curse. Rejoice with those who rejoice, mourn with those who mourn. Live in harmony with one another. Do not be proud, but be willing to associate with people of low position. Do not be conceited.
>
> Do not repay anyone evil for evil. Be careful to do what is right in the eyes of everybody. If it is possible, as far as it depends on you, live at peace with everyone (Romans 12:9–18).

This passage requires a commitment from Christians to bless all people, enemy or not, and to offer them hospitality. This has profound implications for Christians and international relations.

Both Christianity and feminism problematize power because it is ruthless, manipulative, and certainly not humble. Chapter 1, "Harming Others," explores feminist and gender studies criticisms of international relations. Specifically, it defines hegemonic Christianity, based upon the concept of hegemonic masculinity. Hegemonic Christians are convinced of their own theological faultlessness to the detriment of hearing and valuing other Christian perspectives. This constructs a hierarchy between the different theological strands—creating a hegemon and subalterns. The subalterns include differing Christian voices and any non-Christian voices that present challenges to the hegemon. It is a distinctly inhospitable structure. Political theologies on war compose a particular hegemonic structure—between themselves and voices on the margins. This results in the inability of these political theologies to account for the security of vulnerable populations. By being so invested in state-centric human constructions of power, political theologians Reinhold Niebuhr, Stanley Hauerwas, and Jean Bethke Elshtain often fail to account for how marginalized populations are affected, specifically the populations living in or affected by failed state conflicts. Arguing from a human security perspective, failed states present one of the largest current challenges to international relations, as most wars today occur in failed states. Additionally, if Christians are concerned with all peoples' well-being, then those most on the margins matter. Therefore, it is necessary to rectify this omission.

Taking account of these populations means prioritizing a different vision of security than the ones these three theologians often articulate. Chapter 2, "Marginal Wars," explores how human security recognizes the vulnerability of those living within failed states. Conceivably more important than terrorism, failing and failed state statuses indicate significant socio-economic, socio-political, and political-economic weaknesses in a state. These put the inhabitants at considerable risk of physical violence, and also of material, health, and environmental risk. Thus, theologies on war need to better grasp ways of approaching those human security concerns. This is investigated using a case study on Plan Colombia, a development plan articulated by the Colombian government asking the international community, mainly the United

States, for aid. Although Plan Colombia would appear to be an excellent example of proactive last resort, the manner in which the United States manipulated the aid given was (and continues to be) problematic, begging the question, Did this serve the United States or Colombia?

Chapter 3, "Hospitality toward Others," relies upon understandings (or rejections) of vulnerability in international relations. Drawing upon postmodern thinkers Jacques Derrida and Emmanuel Levinas, as well as feminist thinker Judith Butler, this chapter understands that the mutual vulnerability of humanity demands a responsibility toward one another. Hospitality ultimately acknowledges the deep responsibility the self has for others. As a cornerstone of the Christian faith, *agape*'s intrinsic care for others (love of God and neighbor before self) is related to hospitality. Instead of being focused on responses to power solely, which makes one complicit in some way with power, Christians must be able to demonstrate a thoughtful approach to conflict that embodies the grounding of faith in *agape*. Thus, it is necessary to be attentive to how war and conflict have been traditionally conceived of by political theologians, scholars who have often unwittingly denied vulnerability and responsibility to marginalized populations in global affairs.

Chapter 4, "The Invulnerability Myth" focuses on Reinhold Niebuhr's legacy, Christian realism. Niebuhr's conception of how anxiety leads humans and states to seek security is one of the better articulations of human behavior. However, Niebuhr found it sinful that security-seeking behavior might happen at the expense of others. I believe that Niebuhr's adherence to nuclear deterrence during the Cold War reflected his desire to promote peace. Yet while nuclear deterrence worked well for the United States and the Soviet Union during the Cold War, it was at the expense of the Third World, as it was referred to in this era. This is a troubling abstraction of the effects of power on the part of Niebuhr. In effect, the policy of nuclear deterrence valued the populations of the United States over the populations of the Third World. This chapter argues that this abstraction of power continues, perpetuating the denial of other people's vulnerability. In order to redress the problems within Christian realism, this dynamic must be overcome by accepting some form of vulnerability along with the provision of security.

Chapter 5, "The Presence of Suffering," begins by arguing that pacifism does not equate with passivity toward war. Instead, it provides an alternative to war—one that is proactive in addressing the needs and hurts in the world. Inherent in Mahatma Gandhi's approach to nonviolence is empathy; Gandhi argued that nonviolent resisters must know and understand—be empathetic to—the other's desires. Such an idea accepts a certain level of vulnerability. Yet the most prominent contemporary American Christian pacifist, Stanley Hauerwas, at his best espouses an often ambiguous commitment to confronting the power structures. Because of this, Hauerwas, while providing a framework for a good alternative, articulates a dualism (church versus world) and the "paradox of privilege" that denies a need to do something about the vulnerability problem. As both Hauerwas and Marilyn McCord Adams claim Cross-centered theologies, this chapter applies Adams' idea of the church as a worldwide, inclusive entity that saves Hauerwasian pacifism from irrelevance in international affairs.

Chapter 6, "The Offer of Hospitality," interrogates traditional understandings of the term "last resort"—one of the key criteria of *jus ad bellum* in the Just War tradition. Many theological justifications for war, from Augustine to contemporary scholars, are rooted within *agape* because a just war provides a way of loving neighbors—either through interventionist protection or by bringing violators back into righteousness. For many contemporary traditionalists, the performance of *agape* and the decision to engage in war stems from a position of theological contemplation and discipline. One of the most widely read Just War books since 1950, Jean Bethke Elshtain's *Just War Against Terror* builds on an *agape* framework but has significant overtones of imperialism and neo-orientalism. This chapter attempts to reframe contemporary *agapic* Just War around hospitality, especially by changing how last resort has operated.

Last resort is closely connected to legitimate authority. Yet the tension inherent in contemporary international relations between state sovereignty and ethical norms is echoed in the tension between

Christian realism and pacifism. This has allowed realpolitik maneuverings to prevent last resort from functioning. I posit that if realism is being challenged to grant more vulnerability to state affairs, then the Just War tradition and the last resort criterion must also be challenged by taking a more proactive approach to preventing war (via pacifism), especially in failing states. Can addressing the variables that are linked to conflict emerging in failed states stabilize the situation as a truer, more hospitable concept of last resort?

CHAPTER ONE

Harming Others

The purpose of the HBO movie *The Girl in the Café* is to highlight the astonishing disparity of material and health securities between the Global North and the Global South (Curtis, 2005). The main character, Lawrence, a repressed bureaucrat under the U.K.'s chancellor of the exchequer, falls in love with an unknown woman (the girl in the café), Gina, who threatens his orderly world. The backdrop of this love story is a G-8 Summit in Reykjavik, where Gina, as Lawrence's guest, awkwardly and uncomfortably challenges the heads of states on the lack of progress toward meeting the Millennium Development Goals. Gina continues to push her point at the state dinner, where she rather forcefully illustrates that a child dies every three seconds in less-developed countries. After she is expelled from the conference, Gina reveals that she has just been released from prison for hurting a man who killed a child. Lawrence asks, "Whose child was it?" and she responds, "Does it matter whose child?" This vague knowledge is all that is revealed about her crime, and the reason for her uncouth behavior is made known: her feeling of responsibility to children in the Global South is part of Gina's larger ethos—all children are our children. As humans operating in the world, all people are responsible for the growth and well-being of children, of all people, everywhere. Such an ethos commands an understanding of hospitality. Hospitality is the deeply rooted desire to provide someone with their needs as an act of welcome, embrace, and love. How can international relations (IR), as a field focused on security, power, and invulnerability practice hospitality?

Expanding hospitality in IR means searching for ways to (better) provide for the welfare of all people. The focus of this book is to frame failed states and the humanitarian crises they produce theologically. It is intended to challenge political theologians and theologically informed politicians and scholars to grapple with power, conflict, and war in ways not done previously. This means reconceptualizing security, moving from hard security (state power based in military strength and sovereignty) to a broader notion of human security. Redefining security requires thinking in new ways about the acquisition, maintenance, and engagement of power.

A surprising tension exists in American Christian political thought between the Christian realists who are too comfortable with manipulations of power, the pacifists who shun power, and the Just War theorists who justify power's use. This chapter lays the foundation for how these competing strains of Christianity within the United States sometimes fail to see issues outside of their claims, such as the failed states on the margins of international relations. It will do this by presenting a feminist critique of the traditionally masculinized field of IR. However, within each theological tradition there is room for growth and transformation. Each strand believes in the transforming nature of God's power and the gift of *agape* as performed through hospitality.

Abstraction is the modus operandi of political realist IR scholarship. Abstraction occurs when IR scholars focus only on the "state" or the "system" and so dismiss or fail to acknowledge societies, individuals, or other entities involved in IR (see Sylvester, 1999). Feminism, among other critical approaches to IR, has pressed the issue of individuals' security—by saying, "It does matter whose child" is on the other side of the bomb, the economic sanctions, or the damage of underdevelopment. Although feminists have historically addressed the abstraction committed by political realists or security studies scholars, I believe that all three theological strands—Christian realists, pacifists, and Just War theorists—abstract the nature of international relations to the detriment of "the least of us," the people about whom Christians should be most concerned. Christianity and feminism dovetail in their commitment to the marginalized and can thus be used to overcome problematic abstractions.

This chapter will demonstrate how the abstractions by political theologians inhibit the seeking of creative solutions to war. As they currently stand, each strand fails to prioritize the marginalized, making their war policies and prescriptions damaging to vulnerable populations. Such complicity (noncritical positioning) with power can never be undone fully, but it can be mitigated via creative solutions to pressing security issues; hospitality, as a grounded theological and postmodern concept, can transform these theologies, particularly the *jus ad bellum* criterion of last resort.

Sites of Power: Masculinities, Femininities, and Hegemony

Feminist theory and gender studies contributions to IR are extensive and relate to many different subfields, such as security, development, postconflict institutions, and international institutions. Feminism has long been engaged in uncovering how dualities operate as a means and method of establishing power. Specifically this has centered on revealing how the construction of masculinities and femininities serve to create, maintain, and enforce power between individuals, institutions, and entities in society. The ways gender dualities function in IR reveal the way Christian theology on war abstracts the reality of the situation. The commitment to masculinist thinking by Christian realism, pacifism, and Just War theorists detract from the actual effects of war— the suffering, the poverty, the disease and hunger, and the killing—as well as the dimensions of human security. This chapter will broadly critique the three strands by identifying the three leading American voices associated with each, but subsequent chapters will deconstruct them in greater depth, showing both the pitfalls and promises of each representative theologian: Reinhold Niebuhr, Stanley Hauerwas, and Jean Bethke Elshtain.

"Where are the women?" is often the beginning question in feminist IR (Enloe, 1989; see also Steans, 2006; Peterson and Runyan, 2010). Sometimes this is taken literally—Where are women in government, the work place, prisons, or development?—but with greater frequency, especially in postmodern feminism, this is meant figuratively: How are women and other feminized subjects ontologically and epistemologically conceived? Thus, where are women and other feminized subjects in the construction and implementation of IR scholarship, statecraft, and policy making? How are gendered conceptions taken as fact or truth? Understanding how gender is a tool for the construction and maintenance of power is essential.

The designation of male, female, or intersex refers to biological, genetic determinations of sex. The gendering of man or woman (or transgender, transsexual, and/or queer) is social construction. Historically, people have thought feminine and masculine traits to be biologically innate and intrinsic. This assumes that women are naturally emotional, nurturing, and peaceful, whereas men are naturally aggressive, assertive, logical, and nonemotive (Beckman and D'Amico, 1994: 3). Most feminists (among others) would argue that these so-called feminine and masculine traits are actually social constructs used to create idealized types and to constrain behavior (Peterson and Runyan, 2010: 2). As someone grows up in a particular culture/location/space, expectations (norms) are placed upon him/her to develop masculine or feminine traits, depending upon biological sex. Stereotypical conceptualizations of masculinity (as rational, assertive, physical, and competitive) and femininity (as emotional, relational, nurturing, and expressive) have shaped socio-political and socio-economic concerns for millennia.

Looking at how actors, activities, subjects, etc. are gendered reveals power (Peterson and Runyan, 2010: 2). Masculinity and femininity are independent categories but mutually constitutive, and they are defined in opposition to each other (Peterson and Runyan, 2010: 11). When dualities or binaries exist, one is inevitably privileged over and at the expense of the other (Peterson and Runyan, 2010: 38, 62; Tickner,

1992: 7–8). Historically, it has been women and feminized subjects who are marginalized and delegitimized, while men and masculinized subjects have been privileged and protected in public affairs.

The binary of the public and private spheres in Ancient Greece is illustrative. The public domain dealt with business, education, and government, and it was inhabited by the rational, logical, intelligent, autonomous male. The private realm was for the education of small children, domesticity, and care, and it belonged to the emotional, nurturing, less or unintelligent, (inter)dependent female. Transgressions were not welcome—indeed the public and private divisions were seen as moral, virtuous, and normal. Thus, to cross over was to commit a vice. Jean Bethke Elshtain argues in both *Private Man, Public Woman* (1981) and in *Women and War* (1987) that this thinking has shaped how we view men and women.

> [I]mages of public and private are necessarily, if implicitly, tied to views of moral agency; evaluations of human capacities and activities, virtues, and excellence; assessments for the purposes and aims of alternative modes of social organization. Readers will quickly discover that the way in which determinations about the public and the private and the role and worth of each is evaluated will gear a thinker's attitudes toward women. This is one way to put it. Another might be: a thinker's views on women serve as a foundation that helps to give rise to the subsequent determinations he makes of the public and the private and what he implicates and values in each (Elshtain, 1981: 4–5).

So it is that gender shapes where one thinks men and women belong—what jobs they should hold, the wages they should earn, and how their citizenship is valued, especially when it is tied to soldiering (see Elshtain, 1987; Enloe, 2000, 1989, 1983). This has a direct bearing on what nonprivileged actors—women—have access to.

> Gender is material in the sense that even while one's gender is not necessarily rooted in the materiality of one's sexed body, it is

nevertheless embedded in social relations. In any given society, one's gender will influence one's entitlement to concrete resources and will be a crucial factor in deciding not only "who gets what," but also "who can do what" or what one is permitted to "be" in any given society (Steans, 2006: 8).

At minimum, IR has accepted the construction of women as passive, gentle, and peaceful, which influences how we think about the fighting of and participation in war. If men are the soldiers, women are the ones left behind to mourn: women are the "Beautiful Souls" that the male "Just Warriors" fight to protect (Elshtain, 1987). Beyond this, IR values and prioritizes strategic rationality over irrationality (emotions), power and aggression over vulnerability, hard security over human security (see Tickner, 1992: 7–8; Peterson and Runyan, 2010: 10–11, 87–92). This is a hierarchy dependent upon gender as a lens through which we see the world (Peterson and Runyan, 2010: 38). Additionally, gender hierarchy is superimposed upon the state level.

States are often framed as masculine actors: as rational, strategic, powerful, and autonomous (sovereign). Tickner argues that this

> "rationalization of global politics" has led to an antihumanism whereby states, posited unproblematically as unitary actors, act independently of human interests. It is a world in which, as Jean Elshtain, observes, "No children are ever born, and nobody ever dies . . . There are states, and they are what is" (Tickner, 1992: 42).

Masculinized states, and powerful ones at that, are the ones seen as important; interstate wars, state economies, and state power are the focus of traditional IR scholarship. This is problematic: if the personal is political, or international (Enloe, 1989)—then where are the people? Where are human rights? Where is human security? If one were to accept that states are the singular entity in global politics, then the dissident Chinese artist Ai Weiwei would not garner so much interest; Amanda Knox's imprisonment and Meredith Kercher's death would not matter; the U.S. hikers in Iran would have remained there; and

Time would not have made "The Protester" the Person of the Year in 2011. The tsunami in Japan would have no impact on global security (the radiation cloud, ocean pollution, and the future of nuclear energy). Thus, gender analysis allows us to see how these divisions operate and how the divisions impede a true picture of what is happening and how it is happening. Gender analysis allows for a richer, fuller, more meaningful image to materialize.

As feminists and gender studies scholars have expanded upon the duality between masculinities and femininities, they have examined how a hierarchy is created by the competition not just between masculinity and femininity, but between masculinities and other masculinities and femininities. This is understood as hegemonic masculinity, where the dominance of one masculinity at the expense of subordinated forms of the genders (the subaltern) appears to be normal. The process of establishing a hegemonic form of a gender is competitive. The hegemonic masculinity will change depending upon location, structure, time, etc. So what might be the dominant form in one place may not be in another. Arguably, however, there is a global one as represented in "the ideal form of masculinity as performed by men with the most power attributes, who not incidentally populate most global power positions—typically white, Western, upper-class, straight men who have conferred on [themselves] the complete range of gender, race, class, national, and sexuality privileges" (Peterson and Runyan, 2010: 7). It explains how Dominique Strauss-Kahn was dealt with after he was accused of rape and sexual harassment: lightly.

Subordinated masculinities "are embodied by those who lack one, some, or all of these privileges and thus are rendered 'feminized' on those scores" (Peterson and Runyan, 2010: 7). Often these deficiencies intersect with other identifiers, such as race, socio-economic status, and geopolitical location. It is witnessed in what T. R. Carrigan, W. (Raewyn) Connell, and J. Lee (1985) call "marginal men," who are denigrated based on race or sexuality. Further, hegemonic masculinity requires a level of abstraction and idealization of what this form of masculinity should be (and what the other subordinated forms should be as well). Finally, hegemonic masculinity necessitates a level of complicity in how this construction of idealized types creates and maintains power differentials between people and institutions (see Connell and Messerschmidt, 2005; Hearn, 2004; Carrigan, Connell, and Lee, 1985; Bates, 1975). These conditions of competition between different ways of being (which is what gendering is all about), abstraction, and complicity are fundamental to this study.

The gender lens determines what people view as important. For too long, IR has prioritized the rational, sovereign state and the issues a state deals with: power and self-interest. But power is more than state power, and state power affects more than other states. Feminists in IR argue that "to make sense of international politics we also have to read power backwards and forwards" (Enloe, 2000: 196). Cynthia Enloe argues that interstate power relations are not simply war games (Enloe, 2000: 196). Reading power "backwards and forwards" involves grasping how the international impacts lives in a way that abstract conceptions of power cannot get to. Abstraction paints security in broad terms; it occurs when IR scholars and practitioners become wedded to generalizations used to explain various events as discreet units. Abstractions and generalizations avoid details and differences and in the process further widen the gulf between reality and theory (Sylvester, 1999: 34–35). Deabstraction involves us asking, "Does it matter whose child?"[1] Hegemonic conceptualizations prevents us from getting to the goal of fully realized human security because they rely upon the pattern of thought and behavior that inhibits the asking and answering of contrary questions in IR.

The Implications for Christianity

When Christian realism, pacifism, and the Just War tradition focus solely upon the role of hard security or the sovereign state, they are privileging masculinist security concerns at the expense of others. This may be more obvious in looking at Christian realism, which embraces the balance of power as a means of keeping the peace (Lovin, 2007: 57–58; R. Niebuhr, 1962a: 158). The Just War tradition is similar.

Recently, Just War scholars have been criticized for no longer using the tradition as an ethical method for slowing states' decision to engage in war (see Bell, 2009). Instead, critics argue, scholars like Elshtain, have used the Just War tradition for a prescriptive checklist for readily going to war (see Fotion, 2007). It is less obvious in Christian pacifism, but when pacifists, such as Hauerwas, vaguely define war and see state power as a threat to the real peace as afforded by the Trinity (Hauerwas and Coles, 2008: 7, 15, 100–101, 105, 208; Hauerwas, Berkmann, and Cartwright, 2001: 412, 421), they fail to recognize the suffering that occurs when people and states fail to act.

The ugly truth is that Christianity, like all religions and ideologies, creates difference far too easily. When dissimilarities exist, the varying groups compete and use the differences against each other. Distinctions are drawn between churches, denominations, Christians in other regions, and Christians in other countries. Creating and seeing differences between like-minded peoples contributes to seeing even larger differences in nonbelievers. This creates a hierarchy of believers, with believers of a certain stripe against and over believers of another stripe that are both placed against and over nonbelievers. Calling such competition and positioning "hegemonic Christianity" draws attention to how Christian thinking sometimes unwittingly and/or unintentionally participates in the marginalization of people.

Just as there are different forms of masculinity that change and assume dominance at different times, there are different forms of Christianity that are shaped by cultural context and have dominance at different times. (One only has to look at a simple timeline of church history to see this.) And depending on place and time, different traditions, strains, or denominations have been more dominant than others. It should come as no surprise that the early church, with no access to power, was pacifistic, or that contemporary pacifist denominations, like the Quakers or other dissenting churches, are resistant to government and state power. Christianity gained state power when the Roman Empire became the Holy Roman Empire and its leadership needed a way to justify wars (see Johnson, 2005). This was the beginning of the relationship between the Catholic Church and the Just War tradition. Just War remained a primarily Catholic theology until the middle of the twentieth century (see Johnson, 1981: 330). Finally, as the American Century ascended so did Christian realism, tied almost exclusively to mainline American Protestantism (and to Protestants in the waning British Empire).

Power and privilege, such as that which exists in the United States, inhibits critical reflection on power. Direct and unhelpful hegemonic engagements with power are exemplified by: Pat Roberston's call for the assassination of Venezuelan president Hugo Chavez (CNN, 2005); pulpit ministers directing their congregations, with implications of salvation, to vote for specific candidates during the past few U.S. presidential elections (see Garnett, 2006); and the construction of the United States as a nation directly blessed by God, which enables a righteous permissibility toward any U.S. activity as it is seen as ordained by God. The recent publicity surrounding the organization known simply as "The Family" or "The Fellowship" reveals an organization that is clearly hegemonic. As it operates out of Washington, D.C., it sponsors the now-contested National Day of Prayer and believes that any form of power, whether it is a dictator's or an elected official's, is a blessing from God to be stewarded and supported (see NPR, 2009; Franzia-Roig, 2009). A 2009 Pew Forum on Religion and Public Life questionnaire revealed that white, evangelical Christians are more supportive of torture than other populations in the United States. The Pew Forum believes that Christians in the United States tacitly accept a complicit relationship with power due to the persuasions placed upon them by political party affiliations and socio-economic status (Pew Forum, 2009a; Pew Forum, 2009b).

In other words, as privileged and protected people, U.S. Christians have a less critical, more complicit (and complacent) relationship with power. Such ease with power can be read in the three scholars chosen to represent the Christian realism, pacifism, and Just War traditions: Reinhold Niebuhr, Stanley Hauerwas, and Jean Bethke Elshtain, respectively. All three are highly respected American scholars. All also have a place in mainstream culture.[2] Further, as each strand has strong ties to particular denominations, each scholar plays (or played) a role in these denominations, which have specific and indicative relationships with government and the state.

The tension between the three strands is created and witnessed in a sampling of Christian-informed academic texts on war. J. Daryl Charles' book *Between Pacifism and Jihad* (2005) is structured to highlight the tension between those who find war to be inevitable (political realists) and those who do not, pinning a solution on a Just War prescription (see also Stassen, 2005: 289). Pacifists are involved in such competitive maneuvering as well. In his Gifford Lectures, later published as *Across the Grain of the Universe* (2001), Hauerwas declares that "Niebuhr's god is but a reflection of ourselves" and that Niebuhr compromised his faith with his belief in "liberal social and political arrangements" (Hauerwas, 2001: 122, 139; see also Lovin, 2008: 26–27).[3] In their own ways, Niebuhr, Hauerwas, and Elshtain have all given up on the world and in this have claimed to know how the world operates. These claims are major flaws in their thinking.

For example, Niebuhr acquiesces to the world and gives up some element of hope. He claims that humans cannot live out Jesus' teachings, for they are impossible ideals—people are too corrupt. The fulfillment of the ideals taught by Jesus will come only when "God transmutes the present chaos" (R. Niebuhr, 1956: 59). Humanity's innate selfishness and need for self-preservation is brought out in social contexts. This means the ideals presented in Jesus' teachings have little application to political/plural life (R. Niebuhr, 1956: 52). An individual may be reconciled to God "through his resignation to his finite condition," but there is no redemption for "the collective life of mankind" because it enables humans to think of themselves as in control and sovereign over their own lives (R. Niebuhr, 1956: 85).

Niebuhr's pessimism is evident in the published letters between him and his pacifist brother, Richard, regarding China's invasion by Japan in 1932. The purpose of the correspondence was to highlight the different approaches to the conflict taken by Christian realists and pacifists. In the end, Reinhold still concludes that even if his brother has a better grasp of the Gospels, he, Reinhold, has a better understanding of human nature and power (R. Niebuhr, 1932: 41517; H. Richard

Niebuhr, 1932: 378–80). Niebuhr's claim that he knows the true nature of humans denies that God is present and transcendent in the here and now and that God's grace may enable humans to act radically. There is very little room for optimism in Niebuhrian thought. As will be further developed in chapter 4, this pessimism toward human nature leads Niebuhr to make holistic claims about how best to operationalize power, specifically masculinized uses of the balance of power in international politics. This move brilliantly protects the citizens of the United States and its allied countries during the Cold War—even, arguably, the citizens of the U.S.S.R. and the Warsaw Pact countries—while unfortunately leaving those outside these boundaries in a more precarious position. By doing so, Niebuhr is unafraid of claiming and wielding a balanced yet abstracted power that prioritizes state security over human security.

In elaborating upon what he claims to be the social ethic of Jesus (that is, Jesus' life is *the* ethic), Hauerwas argues that the purpose of the church is to be the church, not the state. Christians must be wary of helping to make the nation-state system (what IR refers to as Westphalia or the Westphalian system) work (Hauerwas, 1981: 109). This, Hauerwas argues, is not necessarily a withdrawal of the church from the world, though he argues that there is a necessary dualism between the church and the world (Hauerwas, 1981: 50, 91, 109). But herein lies the problem. The church does not have to hold the responsibility of making the sovereign state system work; nevertheless, this does not absolve the church from being in the world. Yet, Hauerwas sees engagement in the world as a flawed "attempt to avoid the tragic" by someone "who desires to carry out his moral obligations." This hubris leads to and "makes us more susceptible to [tragedy]" (Hauerwas, 1981: 106–7). But Hauerwas does not address how ubiquitous tragedy is. Failure to act on an imminent tragedy creates complicity with it. If we continue with Hauerwas' line of reasoning, Martin Luther King Jr. should never have marched or preached against racism because he might die.[4] But his life and mission are greater than his death. And yes, by acting, we may become more susceptible to acting again and again. And the reality is that neither action nor inaction will prevent tragedy from happening. As will be argued in chapter 5, Hauerwas' shunning of power creates its own problem; this abnegation of power, which says others are unimportant, is a power move in itself.

For instance, to claim that there is a tension between being held to the teachings of Christ and acting on a "moral obligation" (as long as this is not a tenuously defined morality) is peculiar. Sadly, I envision Hauerwas as standing in a corner while a Burmese Buddhist monk is being beaten by a member of the Myanmar junta behind him. Hauerwas prays (a powerful tool, yes) while the monk is tortured. Yet Hauerwas has hands and feet because that is how we were created by our Creator. But Hauerwas does not use them because the work of the church is to pray in those instances (see Hauerwas, 1983: 136–38). Thus, there are some power implications in Hauerwas' decision to act in one way and not another; it might be better to ask how a person wants to be helped instead of deciding which way is the best way to help him or her. For instance, would that monk prefer prayers or direct intervention or perhaps both?

Hauerwas claims that by living the ethic of Jesus' life, Christians act as witnesses, which is a manner of peacemaking, or pacifism. Yet the examples he gives of witnesses—Ella Baker in the United States and Jean Vanier in France—are able to be radical Christian witnesses because of the room afforded to them by living within liberal democracies. Rarely if ever does Hauerwas discuss radical witnesses living in nondemocratic states who really know the implications of living in a state where the government has grown tyrannical and abusive. His failure to acknowledge that Baker and Vanier benefit, as he does himself, from the privilege of living in powerful democratic states indicates his failure to acknowledge the circumstances of the nonprivileged. Hauerwas' inaccurate accounting for power and privilege in liberal democracies first denies his own complicity with power and second denies the complicity of churches in privileged locales.

It may seem more natural to rely upon to Jean Bethke Elshtain's work on feminism, theology, and international relations than to critique it, since Elshtain is a leading IR theorist and a chaired professor of divinity at the University of Chicago. After all, Elshtain at multiple times has written poignantly about speaking out against injustice and the misuse of power. In *Who Are We? Critical Reflections and Hopeful Possibilities* (2000), Elshtain reflects on the two biblical creation stories, particularly the Adamist, or Priestly, account, which says "male and female created he them" (Genesis 1:27; see Elshtain, 2000: 13–18). She uses the version in which God created Adam and Eve simultaneously to illustrate that humans are social creatures meant to live within the *imago dei*. Humans live in "expectation" and in "hope," and these are distinctly communal activities embedded in Christian practice and worship (Elshtain, 2000: 25, 127). The *call* of sociality and community should implore Christians to "name things accurately and appropriately" (Elshtain, 2000: 128, emphasis removed). Christians should be drawing attention to horrific events and the misuse of power. Yet, in spite of these beautiful sentiments, Elshtain's more recent work raises considerable problems.

While Elshtain addresses Western constructs of gender in *Women and War* (1987), she reifies essentialized gender roles as a maternal feminist, arguing a perspective of feminism via the role of women as mothers, without fully recognizing that not all women want to be or can be mothers (see Ruddick, 1989; Gouws, 2005: 199–200). This leads to a larger problem: by reaffirming even while acknowledging the destructive polarity of the male/female gender stereotypes, Elshtain defends a Western construction of power. Elshtain's uneasy acceptance of gender roles enables a Western construction of the Westphalian state system. In fact, this defense of power constructions is perhaps at the heart of a much larger problem with Elshtain's recent work that defends the War on Terror via the Just War tradition (Elshtain, 2004). Elshtain seems to be very comfortable with the hegemonic power of the United States, as she feels it was the United States' moral obligation, as hegemon, to intervene first in Afghanistan and later Iraq (see Elshtain, 2004). Elshtain has become complicit with hegemonic masculinity (where it is acceptable to be a strong woman, but only as long as one does so without challenging the existing system). As such, Elshtain defends rather than critiques abstractions of war and other conceptualizations of power.

There are implications of power in the way each theologian gives up on the world. Niebuhr is committed to ensuring that it is not *his* state (and the elements that encompass it) that is destroyed. By *not* being the one destroyed or held captive by some other state's power, he automatically assigns this fate to other populations. Hauerwas is resigned to destruction—his or someone else's. Yet this is a decision he can make only for himself. To push this resignation as *the* moral choice for Christians is to provide Christians with the understanding they have no other ethical alternatives to the tragedies they are witnessing in the world. Elshtain creates a power-over situation when she constructs Afghanistan, in particular Afghan women, as *needing* rescuing from the Taliban by the United States. These are all polarizing hegemonic stances on what is a very complicated issue—the appropriate response to the use of power in response to injustice, such as intervention in state failure. Ascribing morality to U.S. hegemony automatically blesses any use of the country's power.

The Privilege of Complicity

Privilege inhibits people from seeing the reality of a situation. Scholars critical of hegemonic positioning argue that the marginalized and disempowered (subaltern) see and know more because they have to be more aware of power structures and how they operate (see Spivak, 1988). Niebuhr, Hauerwas, and Elshtain are ensconced in power and privilege, which allows them to comfortably establish hegemonic stances on how Christians should approach power. Their acceptance of power, which is then accepted by their audiences, is complicity. Complicity is best understood as the failure to engage, act, and/or think critically about what one benefits from and is presented with as right, normative, and moral (see Connell and Messerschmidt, 2005; Hearn, 2004). All people are complicit with power in one way or another. Marilyn McCord Adams argues:

> virtually every human being is complicit in actual horrors merely by living in his/her nation or society. . . . [T]his happens even in the U.S., because of the economic and social systems we collectively allow to persist and from which most of us profit. Likewise

complicit in actual horrors are all those who live in societies that defend their interests by warfare and so accept horror perpetration as a chosen means to or a side effect of its military aims (Adams, 2006: 35–36).

Even though complicity is unavoidable, this does not prohibit one from speaking and working against it.

Complicity binds together gender studies and theology. Returning to Nicole Duran's interpretation of the Strongman parable as told in Mark 3 helps to illustrate this point. In this part of the Gospel, the Pharisees are intent on trapping Jesus and have just accused him of being an agent of Satan. Jesus replies with the statement that "a kingdom divided against itself . . . cannot stand. If a house is divided against itself, that house cannot stand" (Mark 3:24–25). He proceeds to make the point that a strongman can only be robbed if he has first agreed to be weakened by being tied up (Mark 3:27).

In most interpretations, the divided house represents Satan, and Jesus is arguing that he cannot be in league with Satan because his performance of exorcisms weakens rather than helps Satan. Further, it is meant to reinforce to the Pharisees that Jesus is indeed the Messiah and that they are either with him or against him. Duran believes that there is an additional interpretation. In it, the Jewish leaders (the strongmen) had agreed to be "tied up" by the Roman Empire, failing in their duties to protect their people. She posited that this story speaks to power—specifically, to those complicit with power.[5] The complicity can be looked at in two ways: (1) the complicity of the Jewish leaders with the Roman Empire, and (2) the complicity of the Jewish community with their leaders and the Roman Empire.[6] Like all parables, the Strongman story has multiple meanings. This interpretation may be controversial to some, but it still raises important questions: What relationship should Christians have with power? Is it something to be used to our advantage or something that we should shun? Or can Christians humbly and mercifully have a healthier relationship with power?

Awareness of injustice through critical thought and action overcomes complicity. And Jesus serves as a model of someone who acted critically "by word and example" by acting mercifully to the marginalized (Adams, 2006: 72). Hospitality offers humble mercy to people in dire need. Just as hegemonic masculinity cannot operate without a dependency upon what it is not (subordinated masculinities and femininities), hegemonic Christianity cannot operate without subordinating both competing Christianities and non-Christians. The main problem with uncritical complicity with power is that it makes even people like Niebuhr, Hauerwas, and Elshtain unable to deal with vulnerable populations outside of the West. This is especially problematic today, when most wars are being fought in the Global South. All three conceive of power as state based, but these wars are not interstate wars—they are intrastate, or civil, wars.

Complicity is a problem of abstraction. As hegemonic masculinity relies upon power (physical or structural) to dominate the subaltern, hegemonic Christianity does the same. Power dynamics will always exist, but how the powerful sacrificially relate to the subaltern is "ethics itself"; it is what Emmanuel Levinas poetically calls "liturgy" (Levinas, 2006: 28). In hegemonic masculinity, the *entire* problem is that the dominant masculinities' privileged existence is at the expense of the subaltern. In hegemonic Christianity, the problem is that whether they are physically abused or not, vulnerable peoples are maligned through willful ignorance of their plight.

CHAPTER TWO

Marginal Wars

Since the end of World War II, the number of interstate wars has declined, but wars within states—predominately Global South failed or weak states—has risen steadily, especially in the decade after the Cold War's end. While the number of failed state events has hit a plateau, these wars must still be viewed as a global security threat. Such states have lost their monopoly on violence (meaning the governments of these states are no longer the only organizations with access to weaponry), and their ability to effectively govern and protect their citizens (Rotberg, 2010; *Foreign Policy*, 2010a). These conditions place the people who live in these states at enormous personal risk. Furthermore, failed state conflicts create regional instability through transboundary conflict spillover and refugee migration (Pottebaum, 2005; Ottaway and Mair, 2004; Rotberg, 2002; State Failure Task Force, 2000). Yet the language of failed states is also seen as a means of asserting power over weakened states by powerful states out to serve their own self-interest. Such a power dynamic needs to be carefully evaluated and interrogated.

Recognition of internal conflicts and war has grown, and theologies on war need to find a way to address them. For too long international relations scholars and other scholars of war have prioritized the activities of sovereign states. Theologians who study war have done the same—from Augustine's emphasis on legitimate authority to Niebuhr's acceptance of the Westphalian state structure and his defense of American hegemony. This book aims to argue for the expansion of hospitality beyond state borders, especially as a means of addressing human security concerns raised by failed state conflicts. Later chapters will spend more time developing hospitality and its relationship with security issues, but for now, hospitality should be understood as the care and provision for those in need. Hospitality is more than a duty; it is a desire to welcome and care for others. As such, there is a natural relationship between hospitality and human security.

Wars at the Margins

In her 1999 book, *New and Old Wars: Organized Violence in a Global Era*, Mary Kaldor claimed that the nature of war had radically shifted in the post–Cold War globalized era. Kaldor distinguished between "old" wars, which formed the modern state, and "new" wars, which are driven by identity politics in reaction to globalization and rapid liberalization.[1] Other works have joined hers—such as Michael Ignatieff's insightful ethnographic observations from the new war front lines (*Blood and Belonging: Journeys into the New Nationalism*, 1993, and *The Warrior's Honor*, 1998), Amy Chua's *The World on Fire* (2003), and Benjamin Barber's *Jihad vs. McWorld* (1996). But some others did not see anything radically new in Kaldor's observations, claiming that the Cold War obscured wars that actually fit quite well into Kaldor's definition of new war. There have always been wars and conflicts that the discipline has ignored (or been ignorant of). Whether they were irregular wars during state formation, proxy wars during the Cold War, and postcolonial struggles, intrastate conflicts have occurred for longer than just the post–Cold War period (see Kennedy-Pipe, 2000). Yet the dominant theory in IR has been unable to paradigmatically conceive of such wars due to the abstracted focus upon state power. In a similar manner, political theologians who write on war have scarcely dealt with the wars that happen within states. This must change.

Civil wars and failed state conflicts are a significant problem with serious implications for the welfare of the people within them. They are a bigger problem than interstate wars. Between 1945 and 2003, nine out of ten wars were in the weak or failed states of the Global South (Kegley and Wittkoph, 2003). Between 1989 and 2008, eighty-nine civil wars occurred, compared to seven interstate conflicts. At the start of 2008, twenty-seven civil wars were underway (Kegley, 2009: 380). These wars are often described as "failed state events," where the government has lost all control of the country. Failed state events encompass revolutionary wars, ethnic wars, adverse regime changes (such as state collapse, shift from democracy to authoritarian rule, or regime instability), and genocides or politicides (State Failure Task Force, 2000: v). What these statistics do not demonstrate is the severity of the wars, in which mass civilian casualties, gender-based violence, ethnic cleansing, and genocide are common (see Kegley, 2009: 381; ICISS, 2001; Kennedy-Pipe, 2000). As Elshtain implores, let's accurately and appropriately name things: mass graves in Guatemala and the former Yugoslavia, children with missing limbs in Sierra Leone and Liberia, rape camps in Rwanda and Yugoslavia, utter destruction in Chechnya, and genocide in Cambodia, Sudan, Yugoslavia, Rwanda, Sierra Leone, Guatemala, Peru, and more.

The international community has economic and political statistics and variables available to it that indicate where civil wars are likely to happen. In the decade since Kaldor first published *New and Old Wars* (1999), more research has been done on these wars and the reasons behind them. While Kaldor and Ignatieff acknowledge the importance of economic factors in the new wars, they also emphasize ethnic and identity factors. Yet the Greed and Grievance Project of the International Peace Academy has asserted that this clouds the real reasons why these wars continue (not just start). The Greed and Grievance Project underscores the economic benefits certain groups receive by perpetuating wars. Indeed, the economic utility and benefits of war have replaced the "most basic of military objectives in war—that is, defeating the enemy in battle" (Berdal and Malone, 2000: 2). Why can't last resort operate to address these factors as an act of hospitality? A more timely, proactive response to potential sites of conflict is hospitality beyond borders.

The Three Types of Weaknesses

For eight years, *Foreign Policy* and the Fund for Peace have examined the issue of failed states. In 2012, using twelve measurements, they classified 177 countries according to five levels of stability: critical, in danger, borderline, stable, and most stable. The measurements are mounting demographic pressures, massive movement of refugees or internally displaced persons, vengeance-seeking group grievance, chronic and sustained human flight, uneven economic development, poverty and sharp or severe economic decline, legitimacy of the state, progressive deterioration of public service, violation of human rights and rule of law, security apparatus, rise of factionalized elites, and the intervention of external actors (Fund for Peace, 2012).

The ten most unstable countries, from worst to better, are: Somalia, the Democratic Republic of Congo, Sudan followed by unranked South Sudan, Chad, Zimbabwe, Afghanistan, Haiti, Yemen, Iraq, and Central African Republic (Fund for Peace, 2012). The ratings do not indicate whether or "when a state may experience violence or collapse. Rather, they measure a vulnerability to collapse or conflict" (*Foreign Policy*, 2010a). Further, states may make drastic movements in the ratings from one year to the next due to an "elusive indicator," such as Russia's invasion of Georgia. States that are at war may actually rank as better off than states that are not. For example, Zimbabwe was less stable than Iraq on 2010's list (*Foreign Policy*, 2010b). Therefore, the Failed State Index does not declare a state to be failed, since the ratings may or may not indicate the chaotic violence that is often used to define such a significant collapse. Part of the purpose of the study is to provide information to governments "for early warning and to design economic assistance strategies that can reduce the potential for conflict and promote development in fragile states" (*Foreign Policy*, 2010a). Such policies are arguably the function of hospitality in an international setting, and they inform when to practice last resort.

Other studies specify additional, yet very similar, variables. The World Bank's Conflict Prevention and Reconstruction Unit identifies nine variables as indicators of the likelihood of a conflict's outbreak

(Conflict Prevention and Reconstruction Team, 2005: 7). These cover socio-economic and socio-political indicators alike, such as: low per capita gross national income, high dependence on primary commodities exports, militarization,[2] and high youth unemployment[3] (Conflict Prevention and Reconstruction Team, 2005: 6–7). The political indicators include: a history of violent conflict in the past ten years; political instability (which has two components: frequent transformation of state structure, such as a coup, and the breakdown of law and order, such as in a failed state); restricted civil and political rights; ethnic dominance; and active regional conflicts that may create a spillover effect due to refugees and cross-border skirmishes (Conflict Prevention and Reconstruction Team, 2005: 6–7).

These are similar variables as those recognized by the CIA's State Failure Task Force. "Key drivers" in state failure include quality of life, regime type (characterized by a country's political institutions), international influences (openness to trade and/or membership in regional organizations), and the ethnic and religious composition of the country (State Failure Task Force, 2000: v). Of these, the task force determined that the strongest indication of failure was regime type: "all other things being equal, we found the odds of failure to be *seven times* as high for partial democracies as they were for full democracies and autocracies" (State Failure Task Force, 2000: vi, emphasis is original). Additional factors double the odds of state failure: low material well-being as measured by infant mortality rates; low trade openness, as measured by balance of trade; and the presence of regional conflicts, specifically two or more in bordering states (State Failure Task Force, 2000: vi). Further, states with larger populations and with a high population density had a 30 to 40 percent greater chance of failure. Factors with indirect effect on failure were "environmental factors, ethnic or religious discrimination, price inflation, government debt, or military spending" (State Failure Task Force, 2000: vi).

Although the studies do not align perfectly, the issues they all raise coalesce into the three types of weaknesses this study will address. States with the following kinds of weaknesses have a high likelihood of failure:

- **Socio-economic:** These include micro-economic measurements of quality of life issues, inflation, low per capita gross national income, high youth unemployment, ethnic and religious dominance, and high infant mortality rates.
- **Socio-political:** These reflect regime type, militarization, government structure, restricted civil and political rights, regional instability, ethnic dominance (again), and population density.
- **Political-economic:** These factors are macro-economic measurements, such as high military spending, government corruption, openness to regional organizations (which typically start with trade), balance of trade, and dependency upon primary commodity exports.

Not all of these factors can be fully or ably addressed by outside actors—whether those are states, intergovernmental organizations (IGOs), or nongovernmental organizations (NGOs)—and some states will not welcome help in these areas at all.[4] Historically, aid per capita has been consistently low and not without its own power-over issues (Sachs, 2005); therefore, development strategies are not without their fair share of critics. Yet if the international community knows that these factors lead to brutal, horrific, high-casualty wars—shouldn't these be addressed by a wide variety of actors? While the purpose of the State Failure Task Force and the World Bank's Conflict Prevention and Reconstruction Team[5]—along with numerous IGOs, such as the World Health Organization, and NGOs, such as the International Committee of the Red Cross or Médicins sans Frontières—exist exactly for this purpose, there needs to be a much larger, more consistent, and committed recognition that some form of intervention, prior to humanitarian crisis, is necessary for preventing the loss of life and stability.[6] Providing for the people in the states that fall within these categories is the operation of a reconceptualized form of hospitality—hospitality that can fit within larger theological discussions of how Christians should think about war.

Whereas Christian realists may approach power and war games too readily, pacifists may be too resistant to the use of violence, and Just

War theorists may be too prescriptive, hospitality infuses all of them. Particularly, hospitable actions can transform last resort, the weakest of the *jus ad bellum* criteria, by helping it to operate proactively instead of coercively and reactively. Proactivity requires a vastly different understanding of last resort. No longer can last resort become important as states are gearing up for war, nor can last resort focus on state-to-state wars. Further, it is going to require a different understanding of security—that of human security.

Obligation and Precarity: Human Security

When the Iraq War ended, in December 2011, most of the news coverage opened with how many lives were lost. How many American lives were lost, that is. Occasionally the reports mentioned how many Iraqi deaths were owed to the war. When Iraqi deaths were listed, the numbers varied, as they had in the reporting of the war. Some measurements have included only the number of Iraqis who died due to direct fire and direct hits; some include how many died due to direct fire and also from disease, malnutrition, civilian conflict, or from war-related injuries—measurements that are included in the idea of human security (see Iraq Body Count, 2011). First, the reports that did not also mention Iraqi deaths clearly demonstrated how different lives are valued and seen as important. Second, the reports that did include Iraqi deaths, but not human security measurements, demonstrated how narrowly security is sometimes conceived. Human security recognizes that people's well-being rests not just on military security but on economic, environmental, social, material, and political security as well. Therefore, human security recognizes that people are vulnerable to more than just military might.

Mary Kaldor also sees a fundamental connection between failed states and human security. Kaldor argues that the development of human security discourse grew alongside the rise of "new wars" in the 1990s (Kaldor, 2007). According to Kaldor, "human security is about the security of individuals and communities rather than the security of states, and it combines both human rights and human development" (2007: 182; see also ICISS, 2001: 15). By combining human rights (which emphasizes economic, social, political, and civil rights) and human development (which includes addressing the daily risks associated with poverty, disease, malnutrition, and material scarcities), traditional notions of security are upended (see Kaldor, 2007: 182–85; Human Development Report, 1994). Further, there are five principles of human security that provide a structure through which various communities can deal with this obligation to other humans. They are: (1) the primacy of human rights, (2) working with legitimate political authority, (3) employing multilateralism, (4) focusing on a bottom-up approach, and (5) encouraging regional involvement (Kaldor, 2007: 184–90).

Some view human security as a natural fit with feminist IR scholarship, as the pairing engages the concept of obligation (Hoogensen and Rottem, 2004). Obligation relates to the notions of respect, dignity, worth, and because of this relationship protection is not just confined to self-interest but expands it to include the protection of others. Judith Butler has termed this sensibility "precarity," which she describes as "the fact that one's life is always in some sense in the hands of the other" (2009: 14). Precarity is recognized only when one acknowledges that he/she is vulnerable and that such vulnerability must be accorded to the other, if the other is to be fully accorded the status of human (see Levinas, 2006). Unless one views populations at risk as less than human, and therefore less deserving of protection, then there is a responsibility to actively promote the total welfare of the other.

Yet even in this recognition of precarity is a power dynamic that is not easily overcome. Placing human rights and development issues within a security discourse allows for a troubling militarized answer to be created (Tickner, 1992; see also Blanchard, 2003). For example, the policies that have been created to support human security remain militarized. The Canadian response to human security was the creation of the Responsibility to Protect (R2P), which uses Just War theorizing to justify an intervention for humanitarian purposes (ICISS, 2001). R2P has now been adopted by the United Nations. The second response comes from the United Nations Development Program document *In Larger Freedom*, which examined the "interrelatedness of different types of security and the importance of development, in particular, as a security strategy" (United Nations General Assembly, 2005; see also Kaldor, 2007: 183).

The adoption of military security solutions to address human security promotes the notion of making others invulnerable through (our) invulnerable power. This is a problematic power-over dynamic that is seen in the worry that designating states as failed or in need of intervention for humanitarian purposes as a neoimperial move (see Gordon, 1997: 962–67).[7] It is a reiteration of masculinized commitments to state's military power that denies the actuality of vulnerability. Perhaps it is instead a stronger position to recognize that vulnerability and obligation exist. Obligation and vulnerability are frequent expectations and experiences imposed on women's lives, often resulting in abuse, exploitation, and lack of access and/or care toward women and other marginalized people groups (Sylvester, 2002; Enloe, 1993). And while many masculinized writings in international relations would deny obligation, the individuality yet interconnectedness of life results in vulnerability. As an actuality and as an academic discipline, international relations are determined by obligation and interdependence. This is why expanding the idea of security to include more than just hard power is so important—and why hard power solutions are not always enough.

Human security recognizes vulnerability and precarity and thus the obligation of one to another. Further, most of the scholarship on obligation acknowledges the power problems of acting on another's behalf. Butler (2009) and Levinas (2006) keep this power dynamic in check in part because they see how vulnerability is mutual and in part because obligation is an obsession with doing what is good for others (Levinas, 2006: 64). Those who govern powerful states are apt to point out what is wrong with weaker states without recognizing their own problems or problems of their own creation. This contributes to a subaltern fear of dominance. The Global North/West does not often construct itself as the entity in need or recognize itself as the entity in possession of a troubled relationship with wealth distribution, gender equality, or human rights—even though there is ample evidence to point to this. By acknowledging its own vulnerabilities, the Global North/West could make it more palatable for other regions to accept the help of the powerful.

Plan Colombia: A Chance to Offer Hospitality

Colombia may present one of the better situations through which to establish the complexities of state failure and a form of proactive last resort. Since the Failed State Index was created, Colombia has steadily improved. In the first year of the index, 2005, Colombia was at its worst and came in at 14. The next year its standing dramatically improved to 27. It placed at 52 in 2012 (Fund for Peace, 2012). This indicates that the implementation of Plan Colombia in 1999 was effective. Plan Colombia, introduced by President Andrés Pastrana in 1998, was an appeal to the international community, mainly the United States, to create a Marshall Plan for Colombia to help stabilize the country. Plan Colombia is, in effect, a form of proactive last resort, albeit an imperfect one.

While never entering a full-scale civil war, Colombia has verged on becoming a failed state for decades. In 2000, the government controlled only about 60 percent of Colombian territory (Marcella, 2003: 8, 16). (The Heritage Foundation claims that it held only 30 percent [Johnson, 2001].) Narcoterrorism, using children as soldiers, kidnappings, murder, extreme poverty, and human rights violations by government forces added to increasing instability. The conditions of this instability are made more apparent by looking at them in their historical context, leading up to 2000—just after Plan Colombia was introduced—in terms of the three types of weaknesses described above.

Socio-Economic Weaknesses
With a population of 43 million and a GDP of $90 billion, 27.1 percent of Colombians lived off of $1 a day, and 54.8 percent lived off of

$2 a day (Marcella, 2003: 10). Seventy percent of the population lived in urban areas. Unemployment hovered around 20 percent (Cooper, 2001). Urban poverty accounted for entry into the drug trade, and rural poverty accounted for itinerant farmers' decisions to grow coca (Johnson, 2001). Part of Plan Colombia was to help resuscitate the country from a years-long recession (Marcella, 2003; Cooper, 2001).

Socio-Political Weaknesses

Conflict in Colombia is endemic and has been since at least 1948. "La Violencia" started with the murder of a popular presidential candidate, which led to riots that lasted into the 1960s (Cooper, 2001). In the first decade of La Violencia, 200,000 people were killed (Marcella, 2003: 7), making it one of the most brutal of the "dirty wars"[8] in Latin American history. And while the period of instability known as La Violencia ended in the late 1950s, stability has not been restored and the violence has continued to the present day. The left-wing Marxist groups FARC (the Revolutionary Armed Forces of Colombia) and the ELN (National Liberation Army) grew out of a need for self-defense in the late 1960s. As of 2000, FARC had about 18,000 members and the ELN 3,000, and while they, along with right-wing paramilitaries, controlled large swaths of Colombian territory, they enjoy little popular support—about 2 to 4 percent. Both are now considered narco-terrorist groups and command a considerable amount of the narcotics trade (Marcella, 2003: 9; Cooper, 2001). The guerrilla groups earned roughly $75 million a month from the trade (Johnson, 2001).

The right-wing paramilitaries have close ties with the government and the military, and they operate against the left-wing groups when and where the military is unable to do so. Paramilitary forces numbered roughly 11,000 troops. The largest is the AUC (United Self-Defense Forces of Colombia), which garners about 6 percent of popular support. The paramilitaries are financed by the wealthiest coca barons. Andrew Miller of Amnesty International stated that the Colombian military "has gotten out of directly waging the dirty war, and at the same time there has been a commensurate rise of the size and ferocity of the paramilitaries" (quoted in Cooper, 2001; see also Marcella,

2003). The paramilitaries controlled the northern part of Colombia and vied with the left-wing groups to control access to the Pacific.

Narcoterrorism became a problem during the 1990s after the Medellin and Cali cartels were effectively eliminated. Their demise led to what is known as the "hydra effect"; the vacuum allowed for dispersed gang control of cocaine and heroin production for which FARC became an umbrella organization (Cooper, 2001).

The violence enacted by these gangs, narcoterrorist organizations, and paramilitaries have added up to a significant amount of social violence. Between 1990 and 2000, 35,000 people died due to political violence (Cooper, 2001). In 2001 alone, 150 massacres resulted in the death of 1,500 people (Cooper, 2001). The right-wing paramilitaries were responsible for 90 percent of the violence against civilians (Marcella, 2003: 21). In 1990, 100 people were kidnapped a year. In 2000, 3,706 people were kidnapped. This accounts for 50 percent of the world's kidnappings, leaving Colombia with the title "kidnapping capital of the world" (Cooper, 2001). FARC and the ELN commit 75 percent of the kidnappings and the AUC 10 percent; however, the people taken by the AUC tend to disappear more often (Cooper, 2001). In 2000, there were 25,660 murders—double the number in 1984 (Johnson, 2001). Additionally, FARC and the ELN are both known for forcibly taking male children of indigenous families and forcing them to be fighters, calling their conscription a "tax" (Cooper, 2001). All of this violence has led Ombudsperson Eduardo Cifuentes to state, "What we have in Colombia isn't a civil war. . . . What we have is a war of the armed actors against civil society" (quoted in Cooper, 2001; see also Marcella, 2003: 9).

Finally, the Colombian state has also suffered from considerable structural weaknesses. While never having experienced a military dictatorship, Colombia's militarization is unique. The military forces in Colombia have historically been small. In 2002, there were 60,000 to 80,000 soldiers for a territory twice the size of France. Of Colombia's 6,242 *corregimientos* (districts), FARC, the ELN, and the AUC were in 5,300 (Marcella, 2003: 10). Compared with other states that face internal threats, Colombia's military budget as a percentage of the GDP is small at 1.35 percent—Algeria's is 3.9 percent and Lebanon's is 3.2

percent (Marcella, 2003: 13). Nonetheless, the Colombian army is one of the best counterinsurgency armies in the world, having conducted counterterrorism and counterinsurgency operations for fifty years (Marcella, 2003: 12). As will be discussed later, this is not without considerable human rights violations.

Although traditional measurements indicate a low degree of militarization, there are several major problems with how the military and police operate in Colombia. First, there is a severe disconnect between civil life and the military; civilians and military members interact very little, and there is no civilian oversight of the military (Marcella, 2003: 12–13). Second, the police forces are funded and controlled by the Ministry of Defense. (This is significant even though police presence in Colombia is small. For every 1 million people there are 1,670 officers, compared with 2,000 in Switzerland, 2,500 in the United States, and 7,600 in Uruguay [Marcella, 2003: 18].) Third, the rule of law and the judiciary are very weak, allowing whatever power the military and police hold to go unchecked. This is compounded by Colombia's historically weak executive branch (Marcella, 2003: 14–15).

Political-Economic Weaknesses
For a developing and conflict-torn state, Colombia had a fairly decent GDP per capita in 2000: $2,093. It was the fourth largest U.S. trade partner in Latin America and the eighth largest global supplier of crude oil (which has been especially important since Hugo Chavez came to power in Venezuela in 1999). Yet Colombia suffers from a very weak tax system, and in 2000 it was suffering from a heavy-hitting recession. All of this was set to get even worse if the violence from all sides was not resolved (Marcella, 2003: 19; Cooper, 2001; Johnson, 2001).

Human Security for Stability

The enormity of these weaknesses were set to rip Colombia apart if something dramatic did not happen. When President Pastrana came to power in 1998, he hoped to introduce a peace process, infuse the economy with much-needed foreign direct investment and aid, and use the military to address the narcotics trade. Knowing that the country was headed toward outright failure, Pastrana, working closely with the United States, proposed Plan Colombia, which was meant to address socio-economic ills and the violent insecurities at the same time (see *Plan Colombia*, 1999; Veillette, 2005; Marcella, 2003; Cooper, 2001).

When Plan Colombia was first implemented, Pastrana made his objectives clear:

> The chief responsibility for us in government is to build a better, more secure country for this generation and future ones to make the Colombian state a more effective force for domestic tranquility, prosperity and progress. We need to build a state for Social Justice, which will protect all of our citizens, and uphold all their rights to life, dignity and property, freedom of belief, opinion and the press (*Plan Colombia*, 1999: 2).

According to Pastrana, the key to ending forty years of violence was in addressing the economic problems that plagued Colombia. In addition to creating more opportunities for free trade and foreign direct investment, Pastrana proposed an austerity program (*Plan Colombia*, 1999: 5–6). In tandem with peace negotiations with the guerrilla groups, Pastrana wanted to strengthen the rule of law, the judiciary, the military, and the police forces. *Plan Colombia* also recommended tackling the supply side of the drug chain by addressing production, distribution, sales, asset laundering, and arms dealing (*Plan Colombia*, 1999: 6). He also sought to strengthen civil society and socio-political awareness, which involved "accountability in local government, community involvement in anti-corruption efforts, and continued pressure on the guerrillas and other armed groups to end kidnapping, violence, and the internal displacement of individuals and communities" (*Plan Colombia*, 1999: 6). Finally, Pastrana wished to see extensive sustainable development initiatives, in part to help replace farmers' dependency upon coca crops, but also to protect Colombia's biodiversity (*Plan Colombia*, 1999: 6–7).

Overall, the plan balanced military response to guerrilla violence and the drug trade with the need to strengthen the Colombian state through the rule of law, the judiciary, respect for human rights, and civil society. It valued human security by addressing economic development, environmental protection, and human rights. There is no doubt that Plan Colombia was sweeping and far-reaching. One scholar has gone so far as to call it "audacious" (Marcella, 2003: 40). As Plan Colombia was equated to the Marshall Plan, Pastrana requested a sizeable amount of money from the international community, primarily the United States. Although some of the money would come from Colombia, the total was $7.5 billion over six years (Friedman, 2011). The United States already provided Colombia with $330 million a year in aid. President Bill Clinton approved an additional $1.3 billion in aid, 500 military personnel for local training, and 300 civilians to help eradicate illicit crops, gifting 30 Blackhawk and 33 Huey helicopters to do so (Friedman, 2011). Originally, 45 percent of the budget was for development and the remainder was for the military (Cooper, 2001; Johnson, 2001). However, by the time the United States was done with the plan, 80 percent of the budget was marked for the Colombian military's fight against the drug trade and the narcoterrorist organizations (Cooper, 2001).

Securitized Manipulations

The United States' response to Plan Colombia turned what had been a human security–focused document into a military security operation. U.S. involvement in Colombia has always fit within a political realist paradigm, one of securitized self-interest. Securitization theory argues that security is a speech act, meaning that discourse shapes how security is perceived and thus how policy is constructed (Williams, 2003). Since the Cold War, the United States has constructed various narratives to justify its financial and military involvement in Colombia. To the immediate south of Panama and situated on both the Atlantic and Pacific Oceans, Colombia is geographically strategic as well as a significant regional trading partner (Marcella, 2003: 3, 5). From 1952 onward, the United States has offered steady and stable assistance to Colombia. At first, Colombia fit strategically within the Cold War paradigm; the instability that resulted from La Violencia and then the rise of left-wing groups meant that, according to the Domino Theory, U.S. involvement in Colombia was necessary for protecting democracy and freedom globally (Marcella, 2003: 31).

After the Cold War, the United States needed a new reason to continue its presence in Colombia, and the drug trade provided it with one. U.S. aid to Colombia remained relatively stable until the mid-1990s. Until this point, the United States had been engrossed in ending cocaine supplies from Peru and Bolivia. To the detriment of Colombia, the United States had been very effective. Since U.S.-driven demand for cocaine did not cease, the market found another place for production: the largely ungovernable rural areas of Colombia (Marcella, 2003: 34; Cooper, 2001). Because of this, Colombia was the third largest recipient of U.S. aid, after Israel and Egypt, by 2000. At first, the United States emphasized the drug trade over counterterrorism to approve the Plan Colombia aid package. Yet after 9/11, it should come as no surprise that the Bush Administration and Congress began to emphasize the counterterrorism and counterinsurgency part of the aid package (Marcella, 2003: 34, 38; Cooper, 2001).

It can be argued that Plan Colombia has been successful overall. Murder and kidnapping rates have fallen; police presence has risen; the judiciary and the rule of law are stronger (Marcella, 2009). Yet, one has to ask: At what cost? Massacres and extrajudicial killings are still a common occurrence (Amnesty International, 2011). While much attention has been paid to the connection between the government and the right-wing paramilitaries, it still has not been completely broken (Amnesty International, 2011). In fact, one U.S. military advisor finds that depending upon paramilitaries, as long as they are properly trained, is not completely problematic; it is seen as an effective counterinsurgency partnership (Marcella, 2009; 2003). This suggests a laissez-faire attitude toward human rights violations, as, again, the right-wing paramilitaries are the guiltiest of targeting and abusing civilians. This is compounded by the Clinton Administration's decision to waive human rights investigations during his last days in office—even though there were clear violations of the Leahy Amendment, which is a State Department policy that stipulates that counternarcotics aid monies will not be released if human rights abuses are uncovered (see Marcella, 2003; Cooper, 2001). It is also seen in the release of $30 million in U.S. funds in 2011, when U.S. authorities deemed that Colombia had made enough progress toward ending human rights abuses, contrary to findings from the international community (Amnesty International, 2011).

What this all leads to is a failure to address human security and perhaps a failure to really address the reasons why Colombia continues to be ranked in the bottom 50 failing states. It is undeniable that Colombia is in a far better position than in 1999, but can it be said that this is a sustainable situation? Most of the money thus far has gone toward the government and the military, both of which have significant ties to the paramilitaries, all of which are guilty of human rights abuses. While FARC and the ELN are considerably weaker than they were, the issues that drive people into the drug trade have not necessarily been addressed. Instead, the United States has taken this opportunity to become more intimately connected with a weak state for its own gains. Further, the United States has unsuccessfully addressed one of the key reasons that Colombia struggles with insecurity: the demand for cocaine and heroin. Colombia is the source of 90 percent of the cocaine and 60 percent of the heroin consumed in the United States. But cocaine and heroin would not be produced in Colombia if there were no American demand for them (Cooper, 2001). The United States' failure to account for its own role in Colombia's insecurity is not only irresponsible, it is reprehensible. It situates all of the responsibility in Colombia, permitting the fight against narcoterrorism to be conducted within those borders, endangering the lives of very vulnerable people. For instance, beyond the violence, the eradication of illicit crops through aerial herbicide is a serious health risk to the indigenous and impoverished farmers in the area (Friedman, 2011). It fails to hold the United States and its citizens accountable for the demand of a substance that is very harmful not just because of what it does to an individual's body but because of what it is doing to the people of Colombia.

While Plan Colombia is a form of proactive last resort, which amounts to early and requested intervention into a failing state to stabilize it, it is a last resort absent of hospitality principals. Such an absence allows for a power dynamic to come into effect—Colombia is still dependent upon the United States for aid and dependent upon how the United States chooses to view the conflict. Dependency continues a willful ignorance of Colombia's plight by prioritizing the United States' interests over Colombia's needs. While this is perfectly acceptable within the realist paradigm, it is an abstraction and manipulation of what is best for Colombia—what is best for Colombia is what is best for the United States. Because what is best for the United States is to eliminate narcotics and to stabilize a key regional trading partner, the human security needs of Colombia have been placed on the back burner.[9] U.S. policy toward Colombia has failed to recognize vulnerability, and it has failed to critically evaluate the power dynamics at play.

Recognition

A commitment to human security requires the recognition that humans have a responsibility to each other, both within and beyond our borders. Such responsibility is the catalyst of hospitality, and it involves a recognition based on mutual vulnerability. Comprehending precarity and practicing hospitality can be done in a variety of ways, but most importantly, it must be done with full awareness of power dynamics and without strings attached.

A proactive, hospitable last resort can take a multitude of forms. And since most current wars are intrastate wars, one way to keep the Just War tradition relevant is to create a way for it to address these issues in a more proactive and forthright manner.[10] A proactive last resort might include:

- public diplomacy and open engagement;
- development monies and support with as few strings attached as possible;[11]
- cooperation in domestic laws from one state to another (like those between the United States and Thailand over sex tourism,

child prostitution, and sex slavery, that reduce the likelihood of exploitation);

- holding multinational corporations accountable for human rights and environmental policies, as well as inviting and encouraging them to be responsible for further development possibilities (such as building roads and funding schools);
- understanding that the more states are shut out of the power structure the likelier they are to cause criminal and humanitarian crises (for example, forcing China to seek energy supplies from pariah states); and
- standing by R2P's commitment to "military intervention for human protection purposes" by international actors (mainly the United Nations) (see ICISS, 2001).

However, none of these solutions will be a perfect fit every time for the various failed states across the globe, and all of these solutions must be scrutinized for neoimperialism. Even though the "failed state" label has come under criticism for justifying intervention for neoimperialist purposes, this does not mean that the international community should just ignore such dire problems. Of the success stories of states that verged on collapse, *Foreign Policy* cites two that improved on their own (and were, granted, more dramatic improvements): South Africa and India. But three others, Liberia, Ivory Coast, and Haiti, improved with the help of U.N. peacekeeping forces (*Foreign Policy*, 2010a). By addressing the specific weaknesses in states identified by such studies as the State Failure Index or by such groups as the International Crisis Group, scholar-practitioners of international relations can better prevent conflict and allow peace to flourish using a newer, hospitality-encompassing last resort. The offer of hospitality—true, pure hospitality—should alleviate some fears. The action of hospitality centers on extending care in a manner that is appropriate and respectful of boundaries that limit what can be given and what can be received.

CHAPTER THREE

Hospitality toward Others

One basic problem in addressing failed state conflicts is that abstraction has rendered them unimportant in the field of international relations. While this is changing within the discipline, it has yet to affect political theologies on war. A theological approach to war is obviously normative: finding ways of preventing war, taking nonviolent stances, or finding ways to make fighting wars more palatable to the Christian conscience. Hospitality provides a normative theological approach to failed state conflicts, deriving its importance from how the vulnerable are treated. The lives of individuals and the lives of those in failed states have often been only marginally addressed. While the Christian theologians covered in this book have done a better job of dealing with the lives of people on the margins within their own communities or states—Reinhold Niebuhr as a minister committed to social justice in Detroit, Stanley Hauerwas as an advocate for raising awareness about differently abled people, and Jean Bethke Elshtain as a feminist contributor to theology and IR—they have yet to deal with those on the margins outside of their own states.

Recognizing the vulnerability of those on the margins means accounting for their lives and deaths. Vulnerability is a particularly touchy subject in IR, but it is a central theme in Christianity.

Hospitality operates from understandings of vulnerability as well as *agape*, or "self-giving love," which I discuss below. *Agape* overturns notions of power in relationships because the only power that exists is between God and humans. Therefore, integrating hospitality into IR truly seeks to change the paradigmatic approach to power that has defined the subject for decades.

Vulnerable Humanity

The failure to see others fully—to recognize the conditions they live in or to acknowledge the importance of their security—denies a piece of their humanity. In security discourse, vulnerability is to be avoided. Drawing upon Thucydides' Melian Dialogue, IR scholars are trained to know that vulnerability invites attack. A small island in the Aegean, Melos was vulnerable because of its distance from and unimportance to Sparta, its colonial protectorate. Knowing this, the Athenian generals, fresh from winning the Peloponnesian War, felt assured of the decision to invade Melos. Furthermore, if the Athenian generals passed Melos by or retracted the decision to invade, they would have been indicating a weakness in the Athenian empire in relation to its colonies and enemies, opening it to rebellions from its colonies or to challenges to its hegemony. Michael Walzer highlights how such vulnerability is framed as a wholly unacceptable weakness within the political realist IR paradigm (1977: 4–12).

Yet vulnerability is a part of life; no abstractions of power are ever going to fully rid the world, a state, or a human of vulnerability. Vulnerability is a fundamental human condition and a basic part of Christian theology as witnessed in Christ's sacrifice and humiliation on the Cross. The focus upon and seeking of power in IR attempts to mitigate and/or deny both state vulnerability and human vulnerability. Some of the ways this is done is through the use of power (by political realists) and by the acceptance of war (Just War adherents). Yet these methods provide security for some states at the expense of other states and the populations within them. Both IR as a whole and Christian political theology focused on IR need to deal with vulnerability that is not limited to particular states or groups of people.

Anxiety and vulnerability go hand-in-hand (see Williams, 2011). Anxiety is made worse when a person or a state is vulnerable. The documentation from both sides of the Cuban Missile Crisis demonstrates this. The crisis could have ended very badly, but the persistence of the Kennedy Administration in pursuing diplomatic measures over a military confrontation helped to resolve the crisis. In fact, it is the ideological differences between the United States and U.S.S.R. that led to mistrust and the creation of an anxious atmosphere. This helps to illustrate how anxiety operates. An encounter with difference interrupts how a state, or a person, or persons within a state order the world. The anxiety in the Cold War stemmed from the United States' fear that the Western way of operating would disappear if the U.S.S.R. had its way (and vice-versa) (Kennan, 1947). The discourse in George Kennan's "Long Telegram," later published as "The Sources of Soviet Conduct" in *Foreign Affairs* (July 1947), and the National Security Council's Report 68 displays nothing but a deeply held belief that the United States must make itself invulnerable to Soviet influence and power via nuclear proliferation, alliances, and economic power (Executive Secretary, 1950). The creation of this anxiety and fear of vulnerability is another projection of human nature upon state politics.

Theoretically, without other people, the individual would live his/her life as s/he would like. But when other people enter the individual's world, s/he is forced to grapple with the comprehension that life has fundamentally changed (Peperzak, 1993: 19–20; Derrida and Dufourmantelle, 2000: 5). No longer can the individual see the world in the same way because the world had been ordered ignorant of others. Now this self and the other have to reorder the world, taking account of each other. This is a vulnerable position. Human life is not a sovereign, fully autonomous activity. Thomas Hobbes understood this: life is brutish and short because longevity was dependent upon others. His solution was to access power, denying vulnerability and alienating the self from other actors. But this is not a long-term, fully obtainable solution. Humans are dependent upon other humans for nearly everything—there is no life divorced from others (Levinas, 2006: 29, 64; Butler, 2009 and 2004; Coakley, 2002). Recognition of such dependency automatically denotes the mutual, co-constitutive vulnerability of self and other.

It is actually one of Niebuhr's own arguments that helps us wrestle with how to best handle vulnerability. For him, most, if not all, human activity stemmed from anxiety. Anxiety was an outcome of humanity's recognition that we are neither in control nor infinite (R. Niebuhr, 1964: 168, 174, 185). Human secularists add to this by stating that it is the self's confrontation with others that makes us face our lack of control and our finite nature (Peperzak, 1993: 19–20). In short, vulnerability feeds anxiety, which leads either to creativity or sin (R. Niebuhr, 1964: 168, 174, 185). A creative solution would stay focused on a moral solution: love. Believing that love is unobtainable in broader, political situations, Reinhold Niebuhr argues that justice provides a more universal normative solution (Niebuhr, 1932a; see also Patterson, 2003a: 8). Sin leads to the misuse of power, or injustice, which promotes the self over and against others (Niebuhr, 1964: 190). Although Niebuhr may not land on hospitality as a normative or moral answer to war, it is arguably a Christ-centered, creative solution to mitigating human vulnerability, especially in failed state conflicts.

Recognizing co-constitutive vulnerability necessitates taking responsibility (Butler, 2009: 34, 43; see also Levinas, 2006: 33; Peperzak, 1993: 24), which goes beyond "we are our brother's keeper" to being "the-one-responsible-for-the-other" (Levinas, 2006: 5). This is based not just upon proximity but also upon humans' intelligible and social need to belong (Levinas, 2006: 20–24). The more that humans recognize their responsibility to others, the more their responsibility grows. This results in "[p]ower made of 'powerlessness'" (Levinas, 2006: 24). This acquiescence to powerlessness speaks not only of a level of humility but of a final acceptance that humans are not in control. In both vulnerability and responsibility, the self becomes "obsess[ed]" with the good of others (Levinas, 2006: 64)—it is a "liturgy" (Levinas, 2006: 28).

Yet humans do not have to accord others their vulnerability and therefore their humanity. Failure to recognize the importance of the other leads to a host of social evils including racism, sexism, ethnic cleansing, and genocide (Volf, 1996: 77; see also Barnett, 2002; Zarkov, 1995). Difference is a stigma that enables a dehumanization process to occur, which could lead to structural or physical violence (see Volf, 1996: 67). By devaluing others we avoid having to acknowledge our own vulnerability; this creates a power-over situation. The denial of vulnerability allows one to live in blissful arrogance and false assumptions about security and invulnerability, which is also wrongly extended to homes, locales, or states. But hospitality demands that one accept both the self's and the other's vulnerability. This has profound implications for autonomy (self-sovereignty) and state sovereignty. Sovereignty is a simple reality—someone is in control of the house or the state (see Derrida and Dufourmantelle, 2000)—but it is how the sovereignty is maintained or perceived that is the problem.[1]

Thus, sovereignty issues are at play, and they are not easily resolved. People who have been a part of the subaltern approach vulnerability and responsibility with a certain amount of cynicism and skepticism. For too long, women have been the vulnerable selves in homes and societies—the ones responsible for keeping hearth and home, maintaining men's standards of living, and bearing the burden of nationalism (Coakley, 2002; Yuval-Davis, 1997; Hampson, 1990). Without vulnerability, we can be certain that power dynamics will exist (Coakley, 2002: 35). Insomuch as all people practice vulnerability equally, abuse, attack, or battery would not happen; healthy boundaries between self and others would be respected.

There is another reality to boundaries: we can never know another person fully, and in this acceptance of difference, pure love exists. H. Richard Niebuhr best articulates this:

> Love is reverence: it keeps its distance even as it draws near; it does not seek to absorb the other in the self or want to be absorbed by it; it rejoices in the otherness of the other; it desires the beloved to be what he is and does not seek to refashion him into a replica of the self or to make him a means to self advancement. As reverence, love is and seeks knowledge of the other, not by way of curiosity nor for the sake of gaining power but in rejoicing and in wonder.

. . . Love is loyalty; it is the willingness to let the self be destroyed rather than that the other cease to be; it is the commitment of the self by self-binding will to make the other great (1956: 35).

Boundaries will always exist, but there is a loss of sovereignty that happens at the site of welcome, at the acceptance of vulnerability, in the practice of hospitality.

Life exists because responsibility for the other is present in relationships, as discussed in Richard Niebuhr's quote above. An obligation to others is a large part of this responsibility; it is affording others a place under the sun or the acceptance that all children are our children. This limits our own rights and the fulfillment of our desires. Even if this strand of thinking is primarily postmodern secular humanism (with ties to Judaism), it is profoundly reflective of *agape* theology via the emphasis on the responsibility of living in community along with our obligations to neighbors and strangers.

Hospitality's Place

In *Of Hospitality*, Derrida (in conversation with Dufourmantelle, 2000) highlights the Ancient Greek play *The Sophist* in order to illustrate several of the key principles of hospitality. As a citizen of the state, Theaetetus welcomes Xenos, the foreigner. Both parties experience vulnerability. Theaetetus has made himself and his country vulnerable by welcoming a stranger and granting him access behind the sovereignty-granting barrier of the state. Xenos knows that as a foreigner "he will be treated as mad"—different, stranger, other—because his life, as precarious and vulnerable, depends upon the hospitality of the one in power (Derrida and Dufourmantelle, 2000: 5–9). Xenos constructs himself as the one dependent (childlike) upon Theaetetus' patriarchal (fatherly) power. Xenos recognizes how power and vulnerability are intricately related in his construction and makes his dependency clear by pleading with Theaetetus to "not . . . think of [him] as a parricide," a killer of parents or close relatives (quoted in Derrida and

Dufourmantelle, 2000: 5). Xenos is not just referencing the threat he poses as an unknown entity, but also the powerful role Theaetetus now has in Xenos' life. Theaetetus can either protect Xenos' vulnerability or refuse it and reject him. This illustration relates recognition and vulnerability directly to the welcome of hospitality, and it begins to make allusions to the hospitality of a sovereign, autonomous state.

Hospitality receives its strength and force when it is unconditional (Patton, 2003: 164). Unconditional hospitality is a welcome requiring no response from the one who receives it. It is dependent upon the self's sovereignty, either over body, home, or state. In IR, Derrida posits hospitality as located *in* the sovereign state and thus relates questions of hospitality to the newly arrived stranger—as an immigrant or political refugee. In politics and in a locale that prioritizes safety, unconditional hospitality may not be easily achieved. A tension exists in considering whether a foreigner "should be interrogated and questioned or whether they should be offered unquestioning welcome" (Derrida and Dufourmantelle, 2000: 27–29, as paraphrased in Barnett, 2005: 11; see also Frost, 1996: 7). But how can hospitality in IR, so rooted in classic operations of Westphalian customs and norms, especially the sovereign autonomy of the state, be expanded?

While modern interpretations revolve around proximity and a place of welcome, Christian Reus-Smit (1999) argues that the hospitality offered by Greek city-states was not limited by territorial boundaries. *Xenos* meant not just "stranger" but also "guest-friend" (Reus-Smit, 1999: 49). The Greek city-state's freedom of movement operated more like a regional organization's (such as the European Union), which allowed for more migration between city-states. Thus, those outside of the city-state were to be treated with respect and warmth. Still, hospitality was limited (if not denied) by length of stay if the visitor was from outside of the Greek *polis* or if the state of origin and Greece were hostile toward each other (Reus-Smit, 1999: 50). Such a conceptualization of those outside of these softer borders meant there was little ethical constraint on practicing hospitality beyond those borders as well (Reus-Smit, 1999: 49). These looser boundaries are similar to early Christian practices of hospitality.

Hospitality as the Practice of *Agape*

Christian hospitality began as a "risky venture," where the act of inviting people into the sovereignty of the home could be dangerous (Arterbury, 2007: 20). It is similar to what *The Sophist* depicts: "[For the writers of the New Testament] the ancient customs of hospitality revolved around the practice of welcoming strangers or travelers into one's home while promising to provide them with provisions and protection" (Arterbury, 2007: 20). Because of this danger and the acceptance of it, ancient hospitality was highly political. The activity grew out of a desire to mitigate danger, hoping "a host's abundant generosity might neutralize the potential threat while cultivating the stranger's favor" (Arterbury, 2007: 21). Yet such self-interest came after the act of hospitality—only "after the guests had finished the meal, hosts finally were free to inquire about their guests' identity, home region, and travels" (Arterbury, 2007: 21). Ancient practice also required that guests bring gifts. In the exchange of hosting and gift, both sides "took on the permanent responsibilities of a host and a guest" (Arterbury, 2007: 21). As Christianity grew, the practice of hospitality changed. Hospitality was not necessarily fixed to a particular, sovereign location (Pohl, 2007: 29). Hospitable institutions like orphanages and hospitals became important parts of Christian practice. Slowly, these were bureaucratized by the Roman Empire (Pohl, 2007: 30).

Hospitality requires mutual vulnerability (see Pohl, 2007: 27). The only power that exists in relationships built on hospitality comes from God; power exists equally between host and guest (Arterbury, 2007: 21). Therefore, hospitality goes beyond self-interest—it is a reciprocal, mutually respectful practice required of Christians by God. Through the act of hospitality, Christians transform the locations and the relationships where they practice it. As with ancient hospitality, Christian hospitality is a public activity (Newman, 2007: 12). Christian hospitality stems from worship: just as we are invited to partake in Holy Communion, receiving God's grace and mercy, we are called to open our lives, homes, and places of worship to people from all walks of life

(Newman, 2007: 14). It is a communal activity, stemming out of the *imago dei* and thus from a place of abundance (Newman, 2007: 16). Due to such transforming abundance and owing to a call to provide for others, hospitality can flow only from *agape*.

Agape is a purely selfless, obedient, unconditional love given because Christians have been commanded to love God (Mark 12:30–31), their neighbors (1 John 4:19), and then themselves (Luke 10:29) (Jackson, 2003: 2; Ramsey, 1954). The person who is loving cannot desire an outcome based upon his/her wants, needs, or claims, because a Christian "seeks not his own good, but the good of his neighbor" (1 Corinthians 10:24) (see Ramsey, 1954: 92). Additionally, and significantly for this argument, love is performative because it is "productive" and it "enrich[es] whomever it touches" (Jackson, 2003: 15). All people, the agent and the recipient, share in love, and this enables "human flourishing" (Jackson, 2003: 15). Peace thus flourishes, because although the notion of *agape* is abstract, the practice of it is not.

Agape does not "refashion" the other into a replica of self, but it rejoices in difference, the "otherness of the other" (H. R. Niebuhr, 1956: 35). It grants love to the other for his or her own sake. Even if *agape* continues to abstract relationships between actors, it embraces strangers as neighbors. No longer is the other apart, separate, different by definition, and thus feared. Now, the neighbor, still quite likely apart, separate, and different, becomes a human that the self is commanded to love for the neighbor's own sake (see Ramsey, 1954; Jackson, 2003: xvi). *Agape* brings strangers into community via the self's relationship with God and makes others neighbors; *agape* is *imago dei* performed. For this study, there are two ways in which neighbor-love is transformative: it loves without self-interest, and it loves the enemy.

First, Christians are commanded to love without expectation and without self-interest. Profoundly, they love "disinterestedly." *Agape* is concerned with, not threatened by, the needs and "well-being of the other," which requires an element of "self-sacrifice for the sake of the other" (Jackson, 2003: 10). This is reflected in the H. Richard Niebuhr quotation above. Like the importance of Christ's sacrifice, love "is the willingness to let the self be destroyed" (H. R. Niebuhr, 1956: 35).

Respect for difference and acquiescence to disinterestedness are integral to both *agape* and hospitality.

In IR, the dominant paradigm, political realism, teaches that no action by a state happens or should happen without self-interest because self-interest is key to power. For this reason, security in collectivities is not guaranteed; after all international politics is reliant on justice, not love (R. Niebuhr, 1962a: 158). But does this mean there is no room for *agape*-based hospitality in international relations? Political realists would answer that there is absolutely no room. To act without self-interest is foolish, naïve at best; and to act with someone else's interests in mind is destructive and clouds the issue—it makes one too vulnerable because it prioritizes the neighbor above the interests of the self or the state.

Second, it follows that if Christians love disinterestedly then they do not identify the neighbor either as a friend or an enemy. As Paul Ramsey argues:

> If a person has love for his enemy-neighbor from whom he can expect no good in return but only hostility and persecution, then alone does it become certain that he does not simply love himself in loving his neighbor. If you wish to assure yourself that love is disinterested, you must remove every possibility of requital. . . . If love persists notwithstanding hostilities, then it is in truth disinterested. If, therefore, you wish to prove whether you love disinterestedly, then sometimes pay attention to how you behave toward your enemy (1954: 98–99).

And while Christians are explicitly commanded to love their enemies, *agape* does not rely upon the command. *Agape* is rooted in "'a phenomenon of abundance'" it "springs out of [a position] of strength" (Erich Fromm, quoted in Ramsey, 1954: 104–5). Christians are enabled to love abundantly because they are first loved by God. This love is a gift freely given, and its strength is derived from the gift of Jesus' death on the Cross (Jackson, 2003: 4). Thus, a Christian's strength does not come from what the Christian has materially or has benefited from structurally (whether it is a nice car, personal or national financial wealth, nuclear weapons, or hegemony), but from the vulnerable position and knowledge that God is the merciful, grace-filled Sovereign (see also Coakley, 2002; Adams, 2006).

The selflessness of *agape* is neither completely innocent nor uncomplicated. For generations, women have been constructed to be *too* selfless, and because of that, *agape* is perceived as *too* other-regarding. There is a fear that it invites an exclusive "other-regard or self-sacrifice [that] is not appropriate virtue for women who are prone [gendered] to excessive selflessness'" (Andolsen, 1994: 151). To implore women or other subaltern individuals to make themselves more vulnerable virtually begs mistreatment. Yet in *agape,* it should not be the weak that are made weaker, but the powerful made weak by a desire to serve humbly.

IR scholars are going to be concerned with the security of the state because of the discipline's resistance to vulnerability. But states are not prone to excessive selflessness (indeed states are prone to excessive self-interestedness), and the states that are going to be concerned with giving up power (self-security) are going to be the ones that already possess it.[2] With this conceptualization of *agape*, this book is not asking the weaker states to make themselves more vulnerable. It is asking the opposite—it is asking the powerful states to examine their use of power and to acknowledge an obligation to embrace some level of vulnerability.

How can states that use their power to provide for their security and self-interest (power and wealth) invert their self-interest to disinterest by performing love toward the enemy as a neighbor instead? Might this lead to mutually beneficial interests between neighbor and self, that is, collective security?[3]

As Timothy Jackson argues, *agape* is self-transcendent: "Self-realization comes . . . via interpersonal service that does not look first to personal gain. We must attend to ourselves and our neighbors, but we often care best for ourselves by forgetting the ego and nurturing the other with patience" (2003: 11). War nurtures the ego and often dismisses the claims and needs of the enemy. As an alternative, could *agape* remove possibilities of conflict and introduce possibilities for peace (human flourishing) via the removal of ego (self-interest) and the patient nurturing (aid) of those who might present some sort of threat?[4]

Even if *jus ad bellum* criteria are practiced in conflict, I argue the relevant criterion here is last resort—and last resort measures come too late.

Last resort is practiced currently via arbitration, as quasidiscernment (for example, asking for the backing of the U.N. Security Council). Yet, when arbitration is sought, it is clear that war is already looming. This is not last resort; this is the last warning. It is in contrast to the objective of last resort, which is to hope for a peaceful solution in place of war (Bell, 2009: 189; Fotion, 2007; Lango, 2006). Instead, could states recognize well ahead of time when and where war is a possibility—not imminent, but possible? Scholars of international affairs already possess enough knowledge to recognize where failed state wars are likely; can't last resort be practiced in this instance? This means creating a different understanding of last resort grounded in *agape*'s relationship to hospitality.

Hospitality accepts that all children are our children; it extends across borders, blurs boundaries, and pushes traditional conceptualizations of the Just War tradition's last resort. Without hospitality, the negative side of vulnerability—lack of recognition, need for self-safety above others' safety, and irresponsibility—leads to a rejection of others and a refusal to see their needs. This can lead to violence of all kinds, whether it is physical, structural, or relational.

To Come

Conceivably, hospitality could enable greater security. Some methods for this might include public diplomacy or no-strings-attached aid. These methods would build better relationships between states, which could only lead to greater understanding between states instead of strife. Judith Butler convincingly makes this point:

> The reason I am not free to destroy another—and, indeed, why nations are not finally free to destroy one another—is not only because it will lead to further destructive consequences. That is

doubtless true. But, what may be finally more true is that the subject that I am bound to is the subject I am not, that we each have the power to destroy and be destroyed, and that we are bound to one another in this power and this precariousness. In this sense, we are all precarious lives (2009: 43).

This extends hospitality beyond borders and fits it into a larger definition of last resort. It helps overcome the fearful anxiety. It is grounded within *agape* and alludes to the "responsibilities of moral proximity" (Levinas, 2006: xxxvii). And it is a far different answer than Niebuhr, Hauerwas, or Elshtain would provide. First, it relies less on power than Christian realism. Second, it relies more on power and is far more proactive than Hauerwasian pacifism. Third, it weakens the current conceptualization of last resort to be more proactive than what is seen in traditional interpretations of *jus ad bellum*. Arriving at this answer of last resort may not cohere with all three strains of thought; nevertheless I am indebted to them all.

Mahatma Gandhi argued that nonviolent resisters must be empathetic to the other's desires. Comprehending another's humanity demands that we know or attempt to understand their plight. Christians comfortable in their reciprocal love for Christ should be comfortable enough not only to understand the opposition, but also to embrace it by being empathetic to it. Embracing the self in others means "freeing them from oppression and giving them space to be themselves" (Volf, 1997: 40). Arguably, it is a freeing of the self as well. This is ultimately the practice of hospitality.

Actions without hospitality, without embrace, allow for injustices to be perpetrated. Abstractions become the standard, which permits the student, scholar, policy maker, and the everyday individual to ignore, forget, or deny the realities of war, conflict, and interpersonal violence. These realities cannot be forgotten—not just because catastrophic injustices are happening on a daily basis in places like Guantanamo Bay, Pakistan, Uganda, Sudan, Chad, Burma, and Iraq, but because all peoples are physically insecure, no matter what policies state leaders make and enact. The idea that one is safer because one lives in a developed country with superior military power is inaccurate. It should not have taken 9/11, the Madrid bombings in 2004, or the 7/7 bombings in London to tell the people in the West that they were unsafe, but it did, and perhaps to a limited extent and in a particular context. These events could have led (and might still possibly lead) to activities that could provide greater security for all people instead of leading to activity that caused greater insecurity: the wars in Iraq and Afghanistan. Greater security can be realized after recognizing that military power alone will not protect and provide it.

CHAPTER FOUR

The Invulnerability Myth

Students of international relations often assume that political realists are warmongers, but the truth is that political realists want war no more than anyone else. Ultimately, political realists believe that peace will come through the maintenance of the balance of power. Therefore, they seek power as a means of creating peace through deterrence. This response to the possibility of war and the acceptance of power may acknowledge the existence of marginal populations, valuing them to different degrees, but it certainly does not accept vulnerability. Although the provision of security is important and a central responsibility of the modern state, the way political realism has constructed such security is often problematic to those outside of its immediate realm of concern, such as the developing world in relation to the United States during the Cold War.

While political realism generally has received ample criticism for these abstractions of security, Christian realism has not. Because Reinhold Niebuhr is the leading Christian realist, it is important to examine his failure to truly account for the lives on the margins. This criticism will interrogate pride of power as defined by Niebuhr through Sarah Coakley's conception of vulnerability, focusing on how the pursuit of power contributes to marginalization. Niebuhr is known for engaging paradoxes, which highlights how nuanced his writings are and how difficult it is to make generalizations about his work. The paradox of anxiety and the paradox of the "balance of terror" (R. Niebuhr, 162a: 155) are the ones most applicable to this study of international security. Central to his thoughts on international security is the human tendency toward anxiety, which leads to creative or sinful solutions. The balance of terror paradox echoes the anxiety paradox: nuclear deterrence creates both (creative) security and (sinful) insecurity. Yet, when Niebuhr, against his initial assessments, began to advocate for nuclear deterrence via the balance of terror, he endorsed his own concept of sin—seeking security at the expense of others.

Niebuhr's articulation of balance of power politics and deterrence is at once brilliant and discouraging—brilliant in that he formulates a method for providing for security without war, but discouraging because that method marginalizes those most at risk, people who live in the developing world. Although the state system operates within certain boundaries of international norms, states are inherently self-interested. To prevent warfare, destruction, and the loss of life—in short, to protect its citizens—a state has to engage in some kind of power politics—realpolitik. The only way for a state to maintain security is to attain a certain level of power. The balance of power between two states is the only way, according to Niebuhr, to create justice internationally because the power balance checks the more selfish intentions of a state. Peace is also enabled, according to Niebuhr, through this balance because of the implied deterrence, which uses a state's capacity for retaliation to ward off would-be aggressors. Peace is the ultimate goal of both Christians and realists. Yet in reality, the policies used to create a balance of power during the Cold War made all populations more vulnerable and insecure. Nuclear proliferation meant the world lived with the anxiety of annihilation; the financial cost of nuclear proliferation bankrupted the Soviet Union; and the proxy wars and manipulation of actors outside of the First and Second Worlds exploited those populations.

While Niebuhr does value all humans as children of God and insists upon the absolute necessity of justice, his pessimism regarding human nature and humanity's desire for power detracts from these positions such that the ideal of love falls apart in group situations, and reliance upon power becomes the normative solution to problem solving. That the focus remains on state-to-state power permits and produces an abstract duality between state activities and all else (Tickner, 1992: 4). Where dualistic tendencies are at play, there are varying degrees of access to power. Sarah Coakley links gender dichotomies with how theologians have approached the dualistic nature of Christ. This is particularly relevant when one side, either the divine or the human, gets valued over the other. In this instance, to devalue the human in Christ devalues all of humanity.

This chapter will examine Niebuhr's conception of freedom and anxiety, and their relationship with sin, before explicating how Niebuhr sees the balance of power and deterrence as redeeming security from anxiety. It will then extend the abstraction critique to include Niebuhr and Christian realism. I argue that Niebuhr unwittingly, but nevertheless inexcusably, values states and populations differently, thereby subordinating some groups.

Power and Humanity

It might seem de rigueur to divide political realism into at least three, if not more, subsets: Christian realists, classical realists, and neorealists (or structural realists). These divisions, however, are not nearly as hard and fast as they appear. Drawing conceivably absolute distinctions between the subsets would ignore the fact that scholars and practitioners in each one engage in extensive conversations across the divides. Thus, it may be easy to call Niebuhr a Christian realist, Hans Morgenthau a classical realist, and Kenneth Waltz a neorealist, but all agree on the main assumptions of political realism—that power drives the working of the international system and that justice is achieved through a balance of it.

Nonetheless there are some differences between these segments of political realism. Classical realists, like Morgenthau, do believe that conflict is rooted in human nature, but this is not owed to any theological tradition (see Morgenthau, 1978). Waltz, in writing *Man, State, and War* (1959) and then *Theory of International Politics* (1979), was pursuing a conversation *in* political realism and attempting to correct Morgenthau and others where he thought they were wrong: the source of conflict. It was only as other scholars saw Waltz's assertion that it is the international structure (rather, the lack thereof) that causes conflict as more accurate that neorealism and structural realism became important identifiers. Nevertheless, most if not all of the political realists were in constant dialogue with each other.

Many political realists—including Morgenthau and Waltz—have professed a significant debt to Niebuhr's work—from his scholarship to his pulpit sermons (see Shinn, 2003: 185–90).[1] Therefore, distinctions are made here between varieties of political realism only when referencing the explicit *theology* of Christian realism or when acknowledging the limited purview of feminist criticisms of political realism, which are typically aimed at Waltzian structural realism and not at Christian realism.

Niebuhr was at the forefront of the advent of political realism. In 1932, Niebuhr articulated the idea that socio-political groups are beholden to the complexities of power seeking. This stems from his belief in the fallen nature of humans and thus the impact of sin on social and political situations (Niebuhr, 1932a; see also Patterson, 2003a: 3–6). In his prolific writings, Niebuhr explained why he no longer believed pacifism was an acceptable answer to the power politics of the international system. This was especially relevant as political realism emerged as a reaction against the liberal idealists of the period between the world wars. Along with Niebuhr, E. H. Carr, Herbert Butterfield, and others were prominent political realists. Their main qualm was that liberal ideas had failed to produce a long-lasting peace and instead led the world into an era of totalitarianism and fascism before plunging it into another devastating world war. Their conclusion was that power is the only way wars like World War I and World War II would be prevented in the future (Shinn, 2003: 180–81; Patterson, 2003a: 8–10; Williams, 1986: 293).

The theological underpinnings of Niebuhr's work are what make him so important to this study—no other political realist had as strong a grasp of human nature and how it influences human behavior in socio-political situations. Niebuhr commands respect both within political realism circles and outside of the academic community. He is one of the most influential American theologians, and his work has immediate and direct implications for politics and war. He advised most of the mid-century American presidents while maintaining a presence in the pulpit. Both presidential candidates in 2008, Barak Obama and John McCain, claimed that he influenced their thinking on international politics. In June 2009, Fareed Zakaria, the editor of *Newsweek International*, listed Niebuhr's *Moral Man and Immoral Society* (1932) as the book that tells us "why governments need ethics" (*Newsweek*, 2009: 56). In the academy, a revival of his thinking is being led by Robin Lovin (2008; 2007; and 1995), Andrew Bacevich (2008a; 2008b; and 2005), and Eric Patterson (2003a and 2003b). Precisely because Niebuhr's work is so important to American political theology and because he wrote and spoke powerfully about the transcendent nature of the Trinity, it is deserving of deconstruction.

Niebuhr and Human Nature: Freedom, Anxiety, and Sin

In order to understand Niebuhr's belief that insecurity stems from human nature, one must start with his understandings of freedom and finite human nature. Humans are fragmented pieces of a whole shattered in the Fall. This fragmentation prevents humans from comprehending events as part of a much larger whole: "the will of God" (Niebuhr, 1964: 168). Evil happens when "the fragment seeks by its own wisdom to comprehend the whole or attempts by its own power to realize it" (Niebuhr, 1964: 168). Finite humans must appreciate and be humbled by the infinite, transcendent nature of God's sovereignty. "God's will and wisdom must be able to transcend any human interpretation of its justice and meaning" (Niebuhr, 1964: 168).[2]

It is not that Niebuhr sees humans as evil but that humans have the capacity to do evil as well as good (Niebuhr, 1964: 124). Freedom is the human ability, "the natural capacity," for people "to imagine and to create a new reality in relationship to the limitations from which they have started" (Lovin, 1995: 123). But in this self-transcendent capacity, humans sin and engage in idolatry, because in contemplating power and freedom they forget their limitations and overstate their own importance (Niebuhr, 1964: 164–65). In the freedom that humans are given through free will and independent thought, humans begin to live outside of their boundaries and attempt to transcend their creatureliness (see Lovin, 1995: 132). This leads to the "real evil in the human situation," which is "man's unwillingness to recognize and acknowledge the weakness, finiteness and dependence of his position, in his inclination to grasp after a power and security which transcend the possibilities of human existence" (Niebuhr, 1964: 137). For Niebuhr this is demonstrated by a paradox between Psalms 49 (which speaks about human fear in times of trouble and ultimately the human need to depend upon God) and humans' fundamental interest in seeking security at the cost of self destruction: "the most obvious meaning of history is that every nation, culture, and civilization brings destruction upon itself by exceeding the bounds of creatureliness which God has set upon all human enterprises" (Niebuhr, 1964: 140).

The reality of fragmentation and human inability to attain the highest position of power causes anxiety, which is the origin of both creativity and sin (Niebuhr, 1964: 185). Niebuhr's work most often reflects a pessimistic viewpoint, so it would seem that Niebuhr believed that anxiety leads to sin more often than not (Niebuhr, 1964: 168). Jesus' "injunction" against being anxious is important. It is not humanity's finiteness or dependency that cause sin, but our tendency to be anxious (Niebuhr, 1964: 168). Insecurity in and of itself is neither evil nor sinful, "but [it] becomes the occasion of evil when man seeks in his pride to hide his mortality, to overcome his insecurity by his own power and to establish his independence" (Niebuhr, 1964: 174).

In the anxiety wrought by the freedom and finitude of creatureliness, all pursuits become "infected" with pride, which upsets the harmony of creation (Niebuhr, 1964: 178). There are five types of pride used to mitigate anxiety: power, knowledge, virtue, self-righteousness, and collective (Niebuhr, 1964: 188–203). While all five types are relevant to international security, the pride of power certainly seems to be the most relevant (see Williams, 1986: 293). Niebuhr describes pride of power as taking two distinct forms: (1) humans imagining themselves to be secure, and (2) humans fearing their insecurity and thus engaging in the will-to-power (Niebuhr, 1964: 189).

The first form is "particularly characteristic of individuals and groups whose position in society is, or seems to be, secure" (Niebuhr, 1964: 189). According to Niebuhr, this security is "bogus" in part because it relics upon humans moving beyond their finiteness and in part because biblical prophecy warns those who "rest" in this security "against an impending doom" (1964: 188–89). Niebuhr cites Isaiah, but one can also refer to the minor prophets to see similar themes. The other form, the will-to-power, is due to fearing insecurity, which leads to the sin of "seek[ing] sufficient power to guarantee . . . security, inevitably . . . at the expense of other life" (Niebuhr, 1964: 190, 182). Even if humans are not inherently evil, Niebuhr's pessimism is apparent in this statement that is at the heart of this chapter: that humanity becomes involved in a struggle of human against human. It is anxiety that leads all of humanity to this place, apart from the true security of God's sovereignty (Niebuhr, 1964: 182).

It is at this juncture that the brilliant yet discouraging idea of the balance of power enters. The goal, to preserve peace and therefore life during the Cold War—which after all remained "cold"—was accomplished. This is true only from a narrow perspective, however, since it did not create a true peace; those in the developing world were placed in precarious positions and the arms race put a tremendous burden on the citizens of the United States and the U.S.S.R. Yet, by seeking deterrence through nuclear proliferation, advocates of this policy, like Niebuhr, do not recognize that the monies spent on the arms race came at the expense of others. Further, calling this deterrence between the United States and the U.S.S.R. the "Long Peace" (see Gaddis, 1987) is an abstraction that fails to recognize the death and destruction caused by the proxy wars in places like Korea, Vietnam, Afghanistan, Guatemala, Nicaragua, Cambodia, Chile, Ethiopia, Eritrea, Iran, and

Iraq. Anxiety was also evident in U.S. society, especially as it related to the Red Scare and the rhetoric of the "commie."

God is engaged, compassionate, and concerned with how humans often take on burdens and anxieties that are needless. The sin in anxiety is that it leads humans away from God and denies the power of Jesus' death on the Cross. Christ died on the Cross to carry humanity's burdens (sin). The way Niebuhr formulates a theory of security that is based on mediating and removing anxiety from the situation speaks to his hope to also remove sin from the situation. There can be no denying Niebuhr's brilliance in advocating a secular state policy as a way of retrieving humanity from a place apart from God. Removing anxiety through the balance of power and deterrence allows states and their leaders to provide security without sin, at least theoretically. Yet, because Niebuhr is constrained by the masculinist principles inherent in political realism, such as systematic abstraction, he is unable to consider, even while calling deterrence the "balance of terror" just how much power politics negatively impacts people's lives (1962a: 155).

Freedom from Anxiety: The Balance of Power and Deterrence

> Realistic theology . . . rejects the interpretations that leap from the diversity of beliefs to a theory of relativism, but it must be equally critical of the moral certainty to which religious communities are susceptible. When a religious institution claims "unconditional truth for its doctrines and unconditional moral authority for its standards," it becomes "just another tool of human pride" [Niebuhr, 1964: 201–2]. The consequences of this pride include not only an intensification of conflicts between religious points of view, but an erosion of the religious community's capacity to think critically about its own life (Lovin, 1995: 54).

Referencing the sin of self-righteousness, one of the five prides, Lovin's passage above also reflects Christian realism's recognition of how pluralities function. As a Christian, Niebuhr found no higher concept than the law of love, which is "the law of God and Neighbors as the proper motivation of the will transformed by grace" (Epp, 1991: 5). Yet, love exists only between individuals; rarely can it operate in group settings, and it certainly has no place in international relations. Knowing that there are pluralities of morals, norms, and political persuasions, love cannot be trusted as a value that all humans appreciate equally (see Lovin, 1995: 25–26; Thompson, 1975; Niebuhr, 1932a). In social settings, the concept of love is transformed into justice, which balances all of the competing morals, norms, and persuasions (Lovin, 1995: 26, 70–71; Thompson, 1975: 286). Furthermore, Niebuhr and the Christian realists reduce political behavior to the constant elements of power and self-interest. In political realism, an imbalance of power in the anarchic system[3] leads to war. The best way to construct peace is for power between states either to be maintained or to evolve.

This was all meant to create invulnerability, or at least a notion of it. The balance of power works because it creates a deterrence, or the outward perception of invulnerability. Classic balance of power theory believes the system in question should be multipolar, meaning five or more states should be in a power relationship with one another (Brown, 1997: 108–14).[4] This way, if one state or group of states becomes too powerful, the other state(s) can balance independently or with their allied or aligned power against that state or group. These alliances are meant to be short-term only, and they are supposed to convey fluidity so that power does not become too deeply seated; in other words, alliances should be quick to form and quick to end (Brown, 2002: 109). The primary concern of a state is "the quest for power and security" (Williams, 1986: 293). If a state holds a significant amount of power, specifically a strong defensive or retaliatory force, this deters would-be aggressors. When states make their retaliatory, second-strike forces so threatening to an opposing power, then that oppositional state will not be inclined to risk the possibility of extreme destruction within its own territory or against its own civilians. The rationality of deterrence, which weighs the benefit of aggression against the cost of second-strike, is dependent upon the capability of a defensive, deterrent force (see Sagan and Waltz, 1995).

As a well-respected figure in political realism at large, Niebuhr accepted and contributed to this idea of invulnerability. While, as always, Niebuhr's own thinking was deeply nuanced and highly dynamic (see Williams, 1986: 291; Thompson, 1975), in the end, he advocated both a bipolar balance of power and nuclear deterrence as means toward maintaining peace between the two superpowers, the United States and the U.S.S.R. If Niebuhr had lived at a different time, it is evident that he would have supported a multipolar balance of power, but he was cognizant of the fact that in the post–World War II international climate, that was unachievable (see Ulrich, 2006). Instead, in a world with proliferating nuclear weapons, where two major and opposing forces were left standing, the balance of power and nuclear deterrence were the best—that is, the most realistic—options left, even if they were not ideal.

Any monopoly of power, according to Niebuhr, "generates injustices," which is why democracy, the form of government most favored by Niebuhr, is dependent upon checks and balances (Niebuhr, 1962a: 156). The balance of power within the international system is itself a form of checks and balances and fosters its own form of justice (Niebuhr, 1962a: 158; see also Lovin, 2007: 57–58; Ulrich, 2006: 8), because "new arrangements that achieved the real aims of both sides of old enmities" are constantly being sought (Lovin, 1995: 29). Even though a multipolar system was confounded by the emergence of Cold War bipolarity, Niebuhr found that the United States' policy of containment engendered a form of justice (1962a: 156).

> The prospects for peace are intimately related to . . . the ability of the non-Communist world under [U.S. hegemony] to meet the challenge of so strange and formidable an adversary. World peace requires that the dynamic of this strange political movement be contained, its ambition to control the world be frustrated, and its revolutionary ardors be tamed by firm and patient resistance (1962a: 156).

Further, neither the United States nor the U.S.S.R. could become so secure in its power that it would use it abusively. Indeed, this struggle for international control could lead the United States, because it was a democracy, and therefore apparently bound by some form of morality, to grant foreign aid to countries in need as a means of "competition with the Communist oligarchy" (Niebuhr, 1962a: 157).

The U.S. effort to contain communism rested on multiple factors at the beginning, such as supplying economic aid to Europe and military support to Greece and Turkey, but it became dependent upon nuclear deterrence. Although Niebuhr was troubled by nuclear weapons and viewed the bombings of Hiroshima and Nagasaki as morally reprehensible, he knew that a return to a world without atomic weapons was impossible (Williams, 1986: 294–95).[5] The advent of weapons of mass destruction, especially nuclear weapons, presented Niebuhr with a dilemma: disarmament would mean giving up the means of deterrence (see Niebuhr, 1962a: 155; Williams, 1986: 295–97). Niebuhr described deterrence as the "balance of terror"—in more conventional language, this is known as the "security dilemma" (see 1962a: 155).

What rescues, to a limited extent, states from the security dilemma is both constraint and wisdom joined by the hopeful pragmatism[6] of deterrence (Williams, 1986: 300). After the Cuban Missile Crisis, Niebuhr believed that both superpowers, in recognition of mutual assured destruction, knew that "even a surprise attack would not guarantee victory and would expose the aggressor to a level of destruction which would make the difference between victory and defeat irrelevant" (Niebuhr, 1962b: 24). Nuclear weapons should be maintained only as a deterrent force, and the United States should expand its conventional weapons to alleviate the temptation to use nuclear weapons (Niebuhr, 1962a: 155; Williams, 1986: 302). Again, Niebuhr's nuances are surprising; what was once disquieting—nuclear power—he began to see as somewhat virtuous. He staunchly opposed any form or threat of limited nuclear war—the use of offensive forces as opposed to defensive, deterrent forces (Williams, 1986: 296–97)—but he acknowledged that "by the grace of [the balance of terror] we have a precarious peace" (Niebuhr and Heimert, 1963: 152).

This peace was not enough, nor was it truly peace. Balance of power politics and deterrent strategies are results of the abstraction that realists are accused of, which is based on three assumptions:

1. War is due only to an imbalance of power between states.
2. Militarization and conflict have a limited impact on people's lives and actually provide justice.[7]
3. During the Cold War, *all* international events were related to or had implications for the ideological struggles between the United States and the U.S.S.R.

To illustrate this last assumption, one needs only to examine Niebuhr's approach to the postcolonial Algerian struggle.

While Niebuhr found the French government's insistence that Algeria was "really an integral part of Metropolitan France" to be "fiction," he completely missed the reality of this conflict. Niebuhr constructed Algeria's struggle against French imperialism solely within the Cold War paradigm. His concern with the separation of Algeria from France stems from his doubt that Algeria and France both possessed the "capacity . . . to withstand Communist infiltration" (Niebuhr, 1962a: 160). Thus, he concluded that it was better for both to stay together, denying the Algerians' right to self-determination and reifying France's perceived sovereign right to perpetuate injustice against the Algerians. Niebuhr's explanation ignores the substate ethno-nationalist strains that are often evident in postcolonial struggles. The Algerian struggle, for all of its perceived and professed ties to Marxism-Leninism, had extensive roots within Algerian nationalist identity, as witnessed in the eventual abandonment of secular Marxism-Leninism and the strengthening of Islamism in the independent state of Algeria (see Crenshaw, 1995).

Such an abstract explanation is directly related to post–Cold War criticisms of political realism. When failed state conflicts seemingly erupted out of nowhere after the Cold War, political realists were taken by surprise. Their surprise was a product of hermeneutic ignorance: the conflicts were invisible because they were (1) not conflicts between formal states and (2) outside the Cold War framework of "us" versus "them" (liberal democracies vs. communist totalitarian states, or vice-versa) (Kennedy-Pipe, 2000). Therefore, political realist interpretations of postcolonial conflicts failed to account for movements of self-determination by focusing instead on the zero-sum fear inherent in containment policies—that is, if liberal democracy did not win in Algeria then communist totalitarianism would.

Even though Niebuhr's work acknowledges the importance of all peoples' humanity—for, after all, on both sides of a conflict are children of God (see Patterson, 2003b: 29)—and even though he recognizes the impact of doctrine and ideology on international affairs, he frames the Algerian conflict narrowly and misses the importance of Algerians' choices and ideology. This abstraction is emblematic of what is inherently problematic about political realism: it places prominence on certain aspects, state power especially; it fails to fully account for other factors, such as the postcolonial ideology of the Algerians; and it values certain positions over others. So while Niebuhr certainly acknowledges the importance and power of doctrines and ideologies, he places on them a value below that of state power. This valuing is in part what is behind the problem of othering.

The Fallacy of Invulnerability

Since Niebuhr views the security-taking measures that happen at the expense of others as sinful, it seems natural to examine the concept of the insider and outsider in IR. The construction of sovereign states as the ultimate insiders in IR is "essentially artificial" and completely constructed (Brown, 2002: 21); outsiders (others) are weaker states, non-state actors, and populations on the margins. Yet:

> Political life is impossible, it seems, without some kind of bordering, some distinction between "insiders" and "outsiders." All political entities whether formal (cities, states, empires) or informal (tribes, guilds, universities) find it necessary to distinguish between members and non-members (Brown, 2002: 20).

Because of these seemingly unbreakable constructions, which Chris Brown (2002) argues are not as long-standing as IR scholars like to think, humanitarian intervention, or any intervention into another state's affairs has been largely resisted. It was such constructions that prevented political realists from conceiving of civil wars as anything of importance beyond how they might affect the larger balance of power, further marginalizing the populations in these states. Sarah Coakley and Miroslav Volf are two theologians who wrestle with marginalization and exclusion. Coakley (2002) does not write explicitly about IR, but her examination of power, submission, and othering makes her relevant to my larger critique of Niebuhr's Christian realism. More closely related to IR is Miroslav Volf's work *Exclusion and Embrace* (1996), which he wrote in response to the Yugoslavian conflict and the rise of reactionary identity politics in the early 1990s.

The insider and outsider duality is based upon groups that are constructed in IR to have power (masculinized states) and groups that are not (feminized non- and substate actors) (see Sjoberg, 2009; Gentry, 2014). The focus remains on states, which allows for abstraction, when the alternative is to recognize the other actors at play in international affairs and to recognize how international affairs affect individuals and socio-political groups. There is a deeper duality at play too, one that relates to how we value humanity. Before Coakley is able to address issues of power and marginalization, she works through the duality inherent in conceptualizations of *kenosis* and Chalcedonian orthodoxy. Although an exhaustive examination of both of these concepts is not relevant here, her exploration of how scholars have historically dealt with Christ's dual nature has bearing. Coakley articulates the "'Alexandrian' problem," which concerns how Jesus' human nature is compatible with his divinity and to what degree (2002: 23).[8] This problem emerges in studies of both *kenosis* (Did Christ empty the divine- or human-self?) and Chalcedonian orthodoxy (What does Jesus' dual nature imply? Which role, divine or human, is most prominent? What does this mean for docetism? How do the two natures communicate?).

What is most relevant to this chapter is Coakley's inquiry into analytical philosophy of religion's anti-kenoticism, specifically Richard Swinburne's approach (see Coakley, 2002: 27–30). Swinburne concludes that Jesus' expression of humanness is "in some sense *defective* from its true, heavenly norm" (Swinburne, 1994: 208 as cited in Coakley, 2002: 30). To Coakley, it is Jesus' humanity, in its "frailty, vulnerability," and "self-effacement," that may actually demonstrate to our finite, limited, non-transcendent selves just what "perfect humanity" can be (Coakley, 2002: 30). This directly challenges how "perfect" humanity has been constructed in the West as a rational man—a concept that political realism is deeply reliant upon (whether Niebuhr wanted to acknowledge this or not [see Lovin, 1995: 121]), especially as it relates to how realists construct states to reflect human nature (as discussed in earlier chapters).

When Swinburne denigrates Jesus' humanity, he denigrates all of our humanity, and this allows humans to be seen as less valuable. It is true humans are not divine, but they are valued or Christ never would have died on the Cross, surrendering himself to the horrors of this world (Adams, 2006: 105; see also Moltmann, 1974). In order to move past the fallacy of invulnerability, we must move past this dualism within theology. Coakley, by welcoming in the presence of the divine through contemplation, by asking feminists to reinstate a positive view of submission to divine power, by asking all scholars to reaffirm both the divinity and humanity inherent in Christ, and by encouraging all to abandon dichotomous gender constructions, integrates these dualities. Volf's call for Christians to embrace their own difference also asks them to internalize, and thereby negate, the duality of "us" versus "them" (1997: 41).

One must not only embrace the other, one must also recognize one's place *as* the marginalized (Volf, 1997: 40–41). To Coakley, this means recognizing and embracing some form of vulnerability. Volf argues that it is our vulnerability that leads humans to desire security, but that as humans, finite and violable, we cannot have the ultimate security we seek—this is God's domain (with which Niebuhr, clearly, on some level, agrees). Further, in seeking inviolable security, humans might actually end up as a "danger to others" (Volf, 2008: 3). This is highly reminiscent of Niebuhr's own warning against the sin in security.

Yet this is where Coakley can address Niebuhr. Niebuhr is susceptible to the criticisms brought by feminists against political realists. By regarding state power as the most important, political realists fail to see how power is constructed in substate affairs and how this leaves, purposively or not, groups of people, identity, and social dimensions from holding any place within international affairs—it is an "anti-humanist" perspective (Tickner, 1992: 42). When Niebuhr warned against arrogance in American hegemony, pride in power or morals, or seeking security at the expense of another, he did so constrained by a masculinist perspective dependent on rationality, autonomy, and sovereignty—all concepts that deny the vulnerability of self. Niebuhr was most often concerned with the power that existed between states in balance-of-power politics and nuclear deterrence and rarely acknowledged the individual and sub-state actors' roles in international affairs.

As previously argued, "worldly" power is often considered a masculinist construct. But Coakley argues that in the Foucauldian sense, we all have access to power. There is a "paradox of power and vulnerability" as empowerment comes through vulnerability (Coakley, 2002: 34; see also Volf, 2008). Coakley acknowledges that Christian feminists are wary of vulnerability as a concept because it brings to mind male dominance in its many forms (Coakley, 2002: 33). Yet there is a "danger to Christian feminism in the *repression* of all forms of 'vulnerability'" and the danger would result in "the failure" of "feminists [to] reconceptual[ize] . . . the power of the cross and resurrection" (Coakley, 2002: 33). One might as well replace "feminists" with "realists" or "IR scholars." With a focus on security, Christian realists are also wary of vulnerability. All political realists are unable to deal with vulnerability because they have taken the lesson from the Melian Dialogue that vulnerability invites attack or obliteration. As Niebuhr pragmatically replaces love with justice as a way to mitigate different agendas, he fails to put the Trinitarian Cross at the center (or perhaps simply denies its full relevance). Political realists are, therefore, unable to engage in the vulnerability required to overcome the problems of abstraction.

There is a possibility of empowerment through vulnerability. Vulnerability "is not an invitation to be battered; nor is its silence a silenc-*ing*"; instead, it invites the "'presence of God' . . . a God who neither shouts nor forces, let alone 'obliterates'" (Coakley, 2002: 35 emphasis in original). To deal with this insecurity, political realists argue it is necessary to be the one that *threatens* silence and obliteration (this is after all the function of deterrence). But the possibility of second-strike obliteration risks too much and undermines Niebuhr's own warnings. Coakley's alternative to this dilemma, while again not addressing international affairs, is still relevant: "no human . . . is beyond the reach of either self-deception or manipulation by others" (Coakley, 2002: 36). It is self-deceptive to think we can actually provide enough security for all people and, even worse, deterrence through nuclear proliferation chances annihilation. More than that, nuclear proliferation valued some populations over others. Additionally, deterrence works only between capable states; deterrence is no longer a viable option in a system where state sovereignty is challenged every day by internal conflict, economic scarcities, and political violence.[9]

Coakley argues that vulnerability created through contemplation "up-end[s] [gender stereotypes] in its gradual undermining of *all* previous certainties and dogmatisms" (Coakley, 2002: 37, emphasis is original). Gender stereotypes create a power structure like any other; political realism, with its certainties and dogmatisms, is also a power structure. Political realism and its prized Westphalian international system rely upon the certainties of deterrence, sovereignty, and governmental control. Vulnerability threatens to upend these certainties and the black-and-white functioning of power in international affairs. Thinking that there was certain security in the Cold War ignores the fear present in society and glosses over how close the world came at several points to catastrophic destruction. The false certitude—of state security through power—that existed during the Cold War is long over with the newer recognition of civil wars, the growing attention paid to terrorism, and the advent of loose nukes. Although this chapter and this book are not arguing that world peace would happen through the initiation of serious contemplation by all the world's actors, which is idealistic at best, they are arguing that recognizing that security challenges stem from violations of political and economic injustices on the international, social, and individual levels will move understandings of both soft and hard security into a better place—that is, if state leaders, policy makers, and academics, among others, are willing to contemplate security issues in a far-sighted (proactive) and deeply-sighted (as in, below the international level) way.

Sin: Security at the Expense of Others

Political realism reaffirms a duality that is problematic. At once, it argues that states that seek security are in some ways inviting destruction (Niebuhr, 1964: 140) and that states should build up power as a means of deterrence. Ultimately, political realists actually fear a peace absent of physical and structural conflict. Moreover, Christian realism advocates moral constraints in the international system, which, to its theorists, implicitly upholds some form of Christian norms, but it does so by asking Christian scholars policy makers to think dualistically. These scholars and policy makers must carry Christ in their hearts, but not in their heads. I cannot help but wonder how incoherent it is to ask a Christian to act with humility but to also advocate big-stick policies of nuclear arms races.

The fact that the Cold War did not provide security and justice as planned is reinforced by Robin Lovin:

> [F]rom a realist's point of view, the Cold War rivalry between the United States and the Soviet Union was a good thing. Retrospectively, today's critics question that judgment, morally and politically. They point to the terrible costs of conventional wars in Korea, and Viet Nam and the escalating military budgets that marked the decades of nuclear deterrence between the superpowers. They point to the immorality of threatening nuclear destruction and to the political fragility of the structure of deterrence itself. . . . [In retrospect, we] certainly would not think that the Cold War was a good thing, if we had been just a little less lucky than we were with the results of those nuclear standoffs (2007: 58).[10]

This aptly conveys the naïveté (at best) or the hypocrisy (at worst) of Cold War politics. Sadly, it also conveys a rather large hole in Niebuhr's highly nuanced arguments for balance of power politics and deterrent strategies.

Regarding the Algerian conflict, the world knows now that the conflict had more to do with postcolonial identity politics than democracy versus Soviet communism. But at the time, postcolonial conflicts were seen only in this light. This means the support for banana republics, military juntas, and dictatorships by the supposedly morally constrained liberal democracy of the United States allowed for genocide, ethnic cleansing, and high rates of interpersonal political violence, such as rape, torture, and extrajudicial killings to occur in many countries, including Chile, Argentina, Uruguay, Paraguay, Iran, Iraq, Vietnam, Cambodia, Guatemala, Colombia, and Nicaragua. One may argue that hindsight is 20/20 and therefore this argument is not valid, but the criticisms raised here were being raised at the time as well (see Enloe, 2000 and 1989). Clearly, Niebuhr would not advocate such policies, *but* the Cold War balance of power mentality did because it failed to think more deeply about the true relationship between power and justice.

To an extent, Niebuhr did admit that foreign aid to developing countries, freedom to allow postcolonial self-determination, and resistance to tyranny were all policies the First World should follow during the Cold War (Niebuhr, 1962a: 157, 158). However, all of these were to be limited if the democratic West were somehow seen to be losing to Soviet communism. Selling the idea of foreign aid to a democratic constituency is difficult because of people's inherent selfishness, but to Niebuhr it was imperative for the developed democracies to give, not just so the developing countries could "gain both technical competence and capital funds," but in order to properly compete, to "survive in the contest," against the "Communist oligarchy" (Niebuhr, 1962a: 157). Niebuhr also recognized that self-determination was "a cardinal principle of liberalism" but that the United States could not "afford" to hesitate to intervene in this process if the "social conditions—whether in South Vietnam, South Korea, or possibly, Saudi Arabia—are the kind which invite Communist infiltration" (1962a: 158).

In regard to resisting tyranny, an idea central to the Lockean social contract on which the United States' democracy is based, Niebuhr
valued the democratic *system* itself over and above the people that lived
in a nondemocratic country or weaker democratic countries, which is
decidedly un-Lockean (see Seliger, 1963). Niebuhr advocated for the
United States (and its allies) to be prepared to "encounter defeat" in
regions such as "Asia and Africa" because their "social patterns make
Western democracy irrelevant" (Niebuhr, 1962a: 157). He continued:
The First World cannot risk "any policy which threatens the democratic 'heartland' of free governments in Europe" (Niebuhr, 1962a:
157). Should a country, like "Tunisia or Mexico," have or develop a
"one-party system," the First World should regard it with "sympathy,"
or if a "new nation, such as Ghana, develops the tyrannical and dangerous potentialities of the one-party system," the First World should
be "concerned but not desperate" (Niebuhr, 1962a: 157).

His advice pragmatically surveys the reality of the United States
and its allies finding success in converting these states to the liberal
democratic system. But it undervalues the injustices the people face
within a one-party system or under tyranny, and it values the socio-
economic and political rights and justices of Westerners over and
above those of people in the Third World. The people in Third World
countries, or, more accurately, the states themselves, become important when they offer value to the First World. The countries of the
Third World became important only when their crises (typically humanitarian) could be interpreted as security threats to the First World,
or even the Second. This denies the reality and damage of Cold War
policies.

This mentality is still evident today. The Westphalian international system continues to value the sovereignty of states over other
actors, and within this, to value the powerful over the less powerful.
This insider-outsider structure is evident in the two wars between the
United States and Saddam Hussein's Iraq and in the "Axis of Evil"
label President George W. Bush assigned to Iran, Iraq, and North
Korea. The two kinds of pride of power Niebuhr articulates also
contribute to the dualities in which Christian realism unwittingly

engages. To reiterate, the first pride of power is that an actor imagines itself to be secure. The second pride of power is that the actor imagines itself to be woefully insecure and thus in need of rectifying the situation. Both of these Niebuhr heavily criticized, but he failed to see the connection between them and his own policy prescriptions for the United States

Deterrence is simply imagining security for the state. That it is a figment of the imagination is pointed at by the security dilemma, and it seems even more fantastical in light of the current nuclear era. Thus, deterrence is a construction of security, but not necessarily an actuality. Yet, in some circles, Cold War policies and militarization are still seen as acceptable, necessary, and even uncomplicated. Christopher Gray (1999) seems to agree with Ernest Lefever that the use of nuclear weapons in Japan was "morally justifiable" via the requirements of the Just War tradition. This same reasoning "applies to the nuclear deterrent force developed thereafter" (Gray, 1999: 502). Perhaps even more distressing is Lefever's belief that the Cold War was perhaps advantageous to the most powerful Third World countries because these

> countries used double blackmail against both America and the Soviet Union. Unlike [H. W.] Brands, who is too eager to regard these states as helpless victims, [Lefever] recognizes that "the Christian ethic does not endow the weak with virtue or the strong with wickedness. It calls upon all—rich and poor—to do justice and show mercy" (p. 92). Lefever, who did much primary research in Africa and Asia, holds no illusions about their regimes. He knows that the same states which accused America of brutality often ruthlessly disposed of their own domestic opposition and stole their treasuries blind (Gray, 1999: 502–3).

I hold no illusions that corruption was rampant (and continues to be) in developing countries, but there is also something inherently corrupt about Cold War policies such as Operation Condor and current ones such as the Washington Consensus policies and the International Monetary Fund's structural adjustment programs (see Sachs 2005).

It must be noted that many developing countries are caught between needing to develop and being required to placate the developed world in this process. When states are in dire social, economic, and political circumstances internally, and are being held to international insider standards as an outsider state, it is far too simplistic to claim that these same countries were involved in "double blackmail." Lefever and Gray absolutely fail to recognize the dependency and manipulation the Third World had to deal with during the Cold War (see Ferraro, 1996) and still deals with today.

In the contemporary setting, one also has to recognize the significant changes in this post–Cold War and post-9/11 world[11] (see Gray, 1999). To start, the Cold War period is now considered to be the First Nuclear Age, an age where horizontal nuclear proliferation (across state lines) was fairly limited and the main concern was vertical nuclear proliferation (within a state) (Sagan and Waltz, 1995: 5). When the Cold War ended, concerns became focused on rapid horizontal proliferation. Some states, such as Ukraine, were born nuclear, meaning that they inherited nuclear weapons from the former Soviet Union simply because the territory of the new state contained facilities and silos that previously existed. This concern was compounded by loose nukes, or nuclear weapons that went missing in the chaos of the dissolution of the Soviet Union. These two concerns, along with the fear of dirty bombs and that terrorist organizations would use either loose nukes or dirty bombs, ushered in the Second Nuclear Age. Deterrence is no longer reliant upon the "uncommon [negotiation] skill" acquired by Cold War superpowers (Lovin, 2007: 58). Deterrence was once dependent upon the rationality of a cost-benefit analysis, but in the Second Nuclear Age this is no longer the case. The security proffered by nuclear weapons in the First Nuclear Age was deeply troubling, but it was effective; in the Second Nuclear Age, any notion of security is simply imaginative.[12]

The will-to-power, the second form of the pride of power, is "seeking security at the expense of other life" (Niebuhr, 1964: 182). Cold War policies brilliantly protected the (physical) safety of U.S. and U.S.S.R. citizens, but it did so at a cost to both domestic and foreign policies. Ironically, President Dwight D. Eisenhower is quoted as saying,

> Every gun that is made, every warship launched, every rocket signifies, in the final sense, a theft from those who hunger and are not fed, from those who are cold and are not clothed. The world in arms is not spending money alone. It is spending the sweat of its laborers, the genius of its scientists, the hopes of its children (Eisenhower, 1953).

It was also Eisenhower who launched the Atoms for Peace program at the United Nations in 1953. Yet the arms race in many ways began under Eisenhower. Starting with expenditures during his presidency, the monetary cost of the nuclear arms race to the United States *alone*, as measured in 1998, included $5.5 trillion for arsenal development; $35 billion for maintenance, research, and development annually; and $320 billion for storage and disposal annually (NuclearFiles.org, 1998). This is in stark contrast to the total amount of *all*—not just U.S. or U.S.S.R./Russian—international aid to developing countries in the past fifty years of $2.3 trillion, which amounts to $15 per capita per year over that same period (Sachs, 2008: 47–48). Failed state conflicts often happen in these economically disadvantaged states. Does this not convey that the security provided by Cold War deterrent forces came at the cost of alleviating poverty and, at its broadest, most literal sense, the *true* welfare of citizens in the United States at minimum, but quite possibly the world over?[13] The seemingly brilliant strategy for creating security during the Cold War came at an incredible expense. To Niebuhr, the money was best spent on developing the balance of terror instead of developing countries because those countries, to be colloquially blunt, were not a sure thing.

This begs the question, Where is the justice in this? How is this encouraging the United States to think and act without arrogance as advocated in *The Irony of American History* (Niebuhr, 2008)? How is this at all compatible with the Niebuhr who claimed that those countries that exceed the "bounds of creatureliness which God has set upon all enterprises" bring "destruction upon" themselves (Niebuhr, 1964: 140)? In *The Nature and Destiny of Man*, Niebuhr accuses Augustine of being too identified with the compromised "historic church," thus obscuring Augustine's words "against the pretensions of empire," especially as

> [t]his identification had the merit of introducing a religio-political institution into the world which actually placed a check upon the autonomy of nations; but at the price of developing in that institution [the Catholic Church] dangerous similarities with the old Roman Empire, and of establishing the pope as a kind of spiritualized Caesar (Niebuhr, 1964: 216).

Is this not ironic? Did Niebuhr himself not in some ways become complicit with American hegemony, thus obscuring his own words against the pretensions of hegemony? This irony may be best addressed through yet another reference to Michael Walzer's interpretation of the Melian Dialogue: "Let us have no fine words about justice" (Walzer, 1977: 5). It is power that is important to political realists, not, after all, true conceptualizations of justice.

Beyond Complicity

Even though Niebuhr explicitly argues for humility in Christian realism, whether it is implicit or arrived at via serious contemplation, this seems to be incoherent due to his realpolitik advocations. Both Reinhold Niebuhr and H. Richard Niebuhr argue that recognizing the other in Christian love and hospitality is crucial to those who practice this faith; sadly, within the scope of international relations, relying upon Reinhold Niebuhr for this is not enough. As Christians, we must interrogate issues of complicity with power. In the Strongman parable, Jesus accuses the Pharisees of complicity with empire. Nicole Duran used this parable to make the argument that Christians are not meant to be power-seekers but to be humble. While this is related to

Constantinianism, an idea discussed in the next chapter, it does not mean there is not room to critique Christian realism for not being inclusive of vulnerability.

Christian realists contribute to the understanding that power creates security, but it should be a security that better recognizes vulnerability of self, and more importantly, of others. Pacifism greatly contributes to such thinking. However, contemporary U.S. pacifism is not without its own problems, especially as these relate to privileging the spiritual against the world.

CHAPTER FIVE

The Presence of Suffering

Incorporating vulnerability into IR and into Christian approaches to war is not an easy task. It demands the recognition that human life and state sovereignty are dependent upon one another. Pacifism understands that vulnerability is a constant feature of life, and this requires constant and active care for the marginalized, which will lead to a sustainable peace. Inherent within theories on nonviolence and pacifism is the empathetic embrace of others—to know what another's sufferings and needs are, even so-called enemies. Pacifism is most often associated with a complete rejection of war, and because of this, many international relations scholars gender pacifists as passive and therefore weak (see Charles, 2005: 92). Pacifism is not meant to convey a passivity to war. Instead, it is meant to convey a proactive alternative to war. This requires an understanding of hospitality and vulnerability that most pacifists possess and is necessary for transforming last resort.

Stanley Hauerwas writes beautifully about hospitality, vulnerability, and pacifism. However, he does so in a way that abstracts the reality of war because of his ambiguous dualism of church versus world and his paradoxical relationship with the modern state. Hauerwas claims to live in deliberate tension with and rejection of liberal democracies because of the structural violences they bring. He fails, however, to account for how such states benefit him and how this demands a response from him. This complicity allows Hauerwas to abstract war, making him appear to be wincingly callous about the suffering that exists in the world. Hauerwas' work is dependent upon three dualities: spiritual versus physical, church versus world, and the privilege of the West versus nonprivileged vulnerable populations. To overcome these dualities and redeem his pacifistic commitment to hospitality, I use Marilyn McCord Adams' concept of worldly mismatches and horrors.

Adams' Christology is important because of her understanding of evil. *Christ and Horrors* (2006) makes it clear that evils in the world, such as genocide, poverty, and war, are political, but additionally that all humans, due to birth into the power structures, are complicit with power. These evils necessitate a response from all humans, but particularly from the church, which she defines more broadly than Hauerwas. Comparing Hauerwas' and Adams' Christologies reveals disagreement between the two, but it is Adams' theology that is able to revitalize the necessary proactivity. Before examining Hauerwasian pacifism, it is beneficial to uncover where pacifism's place in IR is. By looking at peace scholarship and activism, Hauerwas' ambiguous commitment to the needs of others becomes clearer. After going through Hauerwas' three dualities, Adams' contribution is elaborated upon.

Pacifism in International Relations

Pacifism is difficult to find in the academic field of IR. It is either considered a personal choice that does not grasp the complexities of power in state politics (see Charles, 2005; Niebuhr, 1986) or it is a way of discussing Immanuel Kant's "perpetual peace" or, more loosely, democratic peace (see Lake, 1992; Herz, 1950). One comes closer to finding pacifism/nonviolence to be a viable option in international affairs in the ever-strengthening field of peace studies. Peace studies is an interdisciplinary field founded on three elements: scholarship, education, and peace activism (Lopez, 2010). And while peace is something of a contested concept,[1] peace studies is often related to idealism and liberal institutionalism and the emphasis each places upon international institutions, such as the United Nations (Richmond, 2008; Reychler, 2006; Lopez and Cortright, 2004; Cortright, 1997).

Peace studies emerged across the globe but was led by Europe and the Scandinavian states as a field of study in the post–World War II era (Lopez, 2010; Ryan, 2003: 75). Whereas IR had until this point focused on the causes of war, peace studies adds to it by examining issues that tend to revolve around local, regional, and global contexts; for instance, questions regarding arms races, the environment, sanctions, children, war elimination, ethnic violence, and peacemaking/peacebuilding/peacekeeping (Lopez, 2010; Barash and Webel, 2008: 2; Ryan, 2003: 78). At its inception, peace studies was immersed in behaviorism, but through the contributions of feminism, environmentalism, and other critical theories, it has become almost universally, unabashedly normative: the aim of peace studies is unequivocally peace (Barash and Webel, 2008: xv; Ryan, 2003: 77). The norms arise from a variety of places, including secular humanism, liberal peace commitments, and various religious traditions. This is a reflection of the relationship between its scholarly and educational facets, along with the expectations of peace activism (Ryan, 2003: 78). Hence, there is an emphasis on practice and activism in academia and upon writings that speak to both, for example, John Paul Lederach at Notre Dame's Kroc Institute, Aung San Suu Kyi's various scholarly articles, and Martin Luther King Jr.'s speeches and writings.

Peace studies works within a human security paradigm, not just by looking at security in a more holistic manner inclusive of elements beyond (or below) military security, but also by acknowledging the importance of many different actors, including individuals, groups, NGOs, and IGOs (Cortright, 1997: xi). This inclusivity moves peace studies away from political realism and a broader dedication to Westphalian, state-centric politics (Richmond, 2002: 4). By including multiple actors in conflict resolution and holding to a different framework for finding peace, the field emphasizes ways to transform conflicted societies based upon the holistic approach of human security (Barash and Webel, 2008: 4; Richmond, 2002: 4; Lederach, 1995). While promoting the importance of international law and organizations, it nonetheless recognizes that these institutions are not unproblematic. For instance, the damaging policies of the International Monetary Fund and World Bank on the Global South or the limitations of U.N. effectiveness in places like Rwanda or Haiti since the early 1990s.

Instances like those are reflected in Johan Galtung's differentiation of "positive" and "negative" peace. Peace is not just "the absence of war but . . . the establishment of positive, life-enhancing values and social structures" (Barash and Webel, 2008: 4). Positive peace is witnessed when there is both civil and inner (personal) harmony; negative peace is evident when civil harmony is accompanied by inner- and/or relational disharmony (Barash and Webel, 2008; 5). Negative peace is quite often related to structural violence, which causes slow and "undramatic" deaths (as opposed "dramatic" deaths due to "direct violence") through the institutionalization of inequalities and inequities within society and structures (Galtung and Höivik, 1971; see also Galtung, 1969).[2] For example, structural violence is problematically embedded in the notion that the world is a more peaceful place, with fewer wars happening now than in the immediate past (see Bova, 2010). Such thinking upholds a negative notion of peace. If the definition of peace is broadened to include the lowered life expectancies of different groups due to structural, physical, cultural, and psychological violences, scholarship and policies should reflect the fact that peace is more elusive than just defining it as the absence of war (Reychler, 2004: 2). The three types of weaknesses—socio-economic, sociopolitical, and political-economic—that indicate state failure and potential conflict reflect this notion of peace.

Peace studies places an emphasis on proactive means for transforming personal, social, and structural conflicts by addressing what is hindering positive peace. A commitment to pacifism/nonviolence is not a presumptive starting point in peace studies, but there is certainly a commitment to finding nonviolent solutions before violent ones. This is an effective strategy based upon normative experience and beliefs. Not only are Mahatma Gandhi, Martin Luther King Jr., and Aung

San Suu Kyi great examples, but nonviolent resistance campaigns for political change have a success rate of 53 percent, as opposed to a 26 percent success rate for armed struggles (Stephen and Chenoweth, 1998: 8). Other achievements include the 2004 Orange Revolution in Kiev and the 2006 April Revolution in Nepal (Cortright, 2010). Perhaps more than war, these examples are the events international relations are made of.

Pacifism is not a token belief chosen when persons feel unwilling to demonstrate a militaristic support of their state (see Charles, 2005). Indeed, this is an ignorant way of regarding what is often a deeply held conviction (Cahill, 1992: 261; see also Elliott, 1980: 27). Pacifism is more than just physical nonviolence; it is an integrated, internalized philosophy that embodies an active commitment to certain normative behaviors, specifically the shunning of physical and psychological coercion of others (Elliott, 1980: 27–28, 32; McCarthy, 2004: 77). Across multiple faith traditions, nonviolence is seen as the practice of love that has led to the politicalization and mobilization of various groups against injustice. This is witnessed in the writings by Gandhi, King, and Suu Kyi.

What ties these groups together is a belief in love—the impossible ideal that according to Niebuhr could never work in politics. Although two of the three examples below ended in assassinations, Aung San Suu Kyi's movement's recent win against the Myanmar junta is amazing. Therefore, these are movements that cannot be dismissed as being without any success at all. Gandhi was clear that love (*ahimsa*)[3] "does not mean helping the evildoer to continue the wrong or tolerating it by passive acquiescence" (Elliott, 1980: 31). Rejection of the injustices committed by those in power is a confrontation borne of love. For Martin Luther King Jr. also, love (*agape*) was a catalyst for action toward change (see King, 1998; Elliott, 1980: 31; Power, 1963: 99). "True nonviolent resistance is . . . a courageous confrontation of evil by the power of love, in the faith that it is better to be the recipient of violence than the inflictor of it" (King, 1998). Aung San Suu Kyi's Buddhism-based pacifism is rooted within the concept of *metta* (loving kindness) and the belief that love and truth (*thissa*) can politically motivate people better "than any form of coercion" (McCarthy, 2004: 76; see also Aung San Suu Kyi, 1995). Even if neither Suu Kyi nor Burma are truly free from the structural and physical violence of the junta, so much international attention is on the situation that the junta must act carefully, and this keeps Suu Kyi safe. Thus, although the situation is not yet resolved, the nonviolence of the dissidents has highlighted the structural violence and the deep injustice in Burma.

In Christianity specifically, *agape* is the impetus behind Christian nonviolence. *Agape* is the ultimate form of hospitality. John Howard Yoder,[4] Hauerwas' mentor on nonviolence, writes:

> I am asked to deal with the enemy people who are the neighbor I am to love. My action must be such as to communicate or proclaim to them the nature of God's love to them. It might be possible to argue that this could be done with a certain kind of force, moral or social or even physical, but certainly it cannot be said by threatening or taking their life (Yoder, 1992: 64).

Yoder takes Jesus' teachings, as does Hauerwas, as normative principles by which Christians can live a coherent life. For Christian pacifists, Christians are commanded to perform and embody *agape*, an act(ivity) inconsistent with any manner of violence (Eberle, 2006: 205). Thus, such a commitment inherently makes oneself vulnerable to the use of power and force by others. Yet, for all of Hauerwas' commitment to nonviolence, his relationship with active resistance for political and structural change is at best deeply ambiguous and at worst nonexistent.

Hauerwas' Blend of Pacifism

Strongly influenced by Yoder, Hauerwas' Cross-centered narrative theology leads him to speak against the corrupting maintenance of worldly power, especially as it relates to the public sphere. Such a focus, however, presents the reader with three related dualities: physical versus spiritual, church versus world, and privilege versus nonprivilege. Like many other Western theologians, he is immersed in a spiritual versus physical dualism that leads to his most commented-upon du-ality, church versus world. In the past, he has been accused of (and has admitted to [Hauerwas, 2001: 234]) creating a church versus world dualism and for failing to engage in the public sphere (Stout, 2005). Arguably, he has dealt with these criticisms, even backing off of a clear church versus world duality in his more recent publications, most no-tably *Christianity, Democracy, and the Radical Ordinary* (2008, with Romand Coles). Still, denied or not, this second duality leads to an ironic third.

As a clear critic of the modern state system (Westphalia) and its dependency on the hierarchical power structure it creates, Hauerwas fails to recognize that his own theology and his heroes' activisms bene-fit from (a) the liberality of the society in which they all operate and (b) the power of the state that enables living in peace. For instance, while Hauerwas says he would be a willing martyr against power, that may never be a possibility because of the privilege of his country of residence. There is a distinct absence and silence in his work sur-rounding those who are killed or martyred daily in places like Nigeria, where the conflict is often seen in religious terms.[5] A duality such as this is, in all reality, a paradox that revolves around the privilege of living in a society where nonviolent witness is a relatively unthreat-ened and unthreatening possibility. Before addressing these larger is-sues, this chapter will first briefly cover the main points of Hauerwas' narrative theology: the formation of Christians, the difference between the church and the world, Constantinianism, the relationship between witnessing and peacemaking, and war.

Hauerwas' Cross-Centered Theology

Hauerwas subscribes to a narrative theology, by which his theology focuses on the stories of Jesus' life in the Gospels. Instead of writing about the implications for an ethical life provided in the New Testa-ment, Hauerwas declares that Jesus' "story *is* a social ethic" and the for-mation of the church must reflect said ethic (Hauerwas, 1981: 37–40, emphasis mine). Because the Gospels are the narrative of Jesus' life, they are the training manuals for how to be a member of the church

(Hauerwas, 1981: 49). All Christian behavior, from the interior life of prayer to an exterior life of witness and service, is to be a reflection of Jesus' life, death, and resurrection (Hauerwas, 1981: 49). It would be remiss not to emphasize the importance of the Cross—the crucifixion and resurrection of Jesus—to Hauerwas' theology. All that Christians are and do hinges upon the centrality of the Cross in their lives (Hauerwas, 2001: 17; Hauerwas, 1981: 44).

Training Christians to follow the narrative of Jesus' life means that the church enables Christians to name what is happening in their lives. All life events are held up to the witness of the church and the narrative of the Cross: "It is in his cross that we learn we live in a world that is based on the presupposition that man, not God, rules" (Hauerwas, 1981: 50). By putting the Cross and the church at the center of their lives, Christians can end participation in worldly power dynamics and claim their "lives as their own" (Hauerwas, 1981: 50). In essence, the focus on the Cross imbues Christians with confidence in God's plan so they can live without fear of death because of their rootedness in the Kingdom of God.

Hauerwas fundamentally links power and the world. Training like this allows Christians to see the world for what it is: a place ruled by power that Christians "hardly know how to name, much less defend against" (Hauerwas, 1981: 50). Worldly powers manipulate humans' "fear of destruction, cloaking their falsehood with the appearance of convention, offering us security in exchange for truth" (Hauerwas, 1981: 50). Remaining focused on the Cross allows Christians to resist such problems. How Jesus cared for and served people in his life and how he shunned power is *the* example for how Christians are meant to do the same. Yet power is tempting and corrupting, and because of this, Christians try to make Christianity necessary to the world by conflating a life of faith and witness with power (Hauerwas, 2001: 221, 224).[6]

Yoder coined the term "Constantinianism" in reference to the conflation of Christianity with power. Leaning on a quasi-accurate historical account of the merging of the Catholic Church with the Roman Empire, Constantinianism is the problematic "attempt to make the church safe by joining its destiny to worldly powers" (Hauerwas and

Coles, 2008: 21). In order to refocus the church on the Cross, the church must "give up claims of political, legal, and social establishment, but . . . more importantly, . . . abandon all attempts to secure the gospel through foundational epistemological strategies" (Hauerwas and Coles, 2008: 21). Thus, Christians are meant to battle the false suppositions of power and control through witnessing and peacemaking.

Living the Jesus ethic as narrated by the Gospels leads directly to a life of witnessing and peacemaking. The importance of the Cross is the narrative of God's love for the world: that he loved the world so much that he sacrificed and resurrected his only Son. God rules the world through transformative love; a rule that is decidedly different from how humans typically chose to maintain power (Hauerwas, 1981: 49; see also Hauerwas, 2001: 211–12). Therefore, it is from the story of God's love that "Christians learn that they are to serve as [Jesus] served" (Hauerwas, 1981: 49). Christians can serve without fear because they are freed from the "threat of death" (Hauerwas, 1981: 50). Christians have both time, because they live without fear of death, and the ultimate power, due to God's awesome, metaphysical, and triumphal power, on their side (Hauerwas, 1981: 48, 50; see also Hauerwas and Vanier, 2008: 46; Hauerwas, 2001: 212). This firm foundation provides for witnessing. If Christians are going to overcome the gap that exists between the church and the world, it is going to be through witnessing. Witnessing is the "'pragmatic' display" of God's redeeming love for the world, and Christians are compelled to witness because "they understand themselves to have become characters in the story that God continues to enact through the ongoing work of the Holy Spirit" (Hauerwas, 2001: 211–12).

Witness is fundamentally related to Hauerwas' conception of pacifism, or peacemaking. Christians and the church confront the world around them through their countercultural witness (Hauerwas, 1981: 105). This may be global, and it should address "matters that matter," but confrontation is valid only if it is Cross-centered (Hauerwas, 1981: 105). Such confrontation is peacemaking by helping "the world find the habits of peace" (Hauerwas, Berkmann, and Cartwright, 2001: 325).[7] However, Hauerwas is also quite clear about what the work of the church is and how it is to be undertaken. Anything that matters must still remain focused within the narrative of the Cross. Christians are called to witness to the world the habits of peace; they offer the alternative of nonviolence to a violent world because they cannot imagine any other response (Hauerwas and Vanier, 2008: 55). This makes Hauerwas' peacemaking and pacifism, like the pacifism discussed at the beginning of the chapter, a creative, imaginative, and "active way to resist injustice by confronting the wrongdoer with the offer of reconciliation" (Hauerwas, Berkmann, and Cartwright, 2001: 325; Hauerwas, 1983: 114).

There is a presumption in the "world," according to Hauerwas, that violence is the status quo and that peace is the exception (Hauerwas and Coles, 2008: 311–12; Hauerwas, Berkmann, and Cartwright, 2001: 325); therefore, war is the human conceptualization of how best to protect self against enemies (Hauerwas, Berkmann, and Cartwright, 2001: 412, 421; see also Hauerwas and Vanier, 2008: 50–51). War, like Constantinianism, is a non-Cross-focused, fear-based attempt to make sense of the world. It denies the narrative the Gospels model for humans, and it is a rejection of the humble servility of Jesus' narrative. War is a coercive tool for protecting and preserve humanity's interpretation of what it means to have a stable existence (see Hauerwas, 1983: 114). War, in essence, is a denial of God's sovereignty over human lives and the world. Therefore, war is "the manifestation of our hatred of God," and peacemaking is submission to God (Hauerwas, Berkmann, and Cartwright, 2001: 421). (I will leave aside this incredible abstraction of war for the moment.) Hauerwas gives some explicit, but rather nuanced, examples of how this peacemaking can be achieved. The following passage does not speak directly to war per se, but it does address what response Christians should feel compelled to make in the face of injustice:

> Campbell and Holloway [civil rights activists] observe that the question, "what can we as Christians, do to help [remedy racial injustices]?" is the question the oppressor demands of his victim. So rather than providing the . . . list [of activities: registration drives, protest marches, petitions, etc.], they quote their friend Thomas

Merton's response to the question of what to do: "Before you do a damned thing, just *be* what you say you are, a Christian; then no one will have to tell you what to do. You'll know." Campbell adds, "Do? *Nothing.* Be? What you are—*reconciled*, to God and man'" (Hauerwas and Coles, 2008: 100–101, emphasis is original).

The above passage speaks against busyness and to the presumption that Christians will always know the appropriate measures of response. Yet there is a certain amount of unchallenged passivity in the statement that American Christians, who rest all too well in their privilege and ease, may feel all too comfortable with. (More on the ambiguity of this passage later.)

The connection between witnessing, peacemaking, and reconciliation becomes even clearer when Hauerwas discusses his deep admiration for Jean Vanier and the community he established at L'Arche. L'Arche was initially a facility dedicated to the needs of people with mental and physical handicaps in France; L'Arche is now an international organization advocating for people with intellectual disabilities. Reiterating that humans have been taught that "violence is the norm and peace the exception," Vanier's respectful treatment and inclusion of typically marginalized people "help us to see that peace is a deeper reality than violence" (Hauerwas and Coles, 2008: 312). Hauerwas also sees L'Arche as the example for Christian political engagement because it is nonthreatening and the very model for visualizing peace (Hauerwas and Coles, 2008: 309–18; Hauerwas and Vanier, 2008: 46). The service and witness exemplified at L'Arche is contraindicative to power; it is the living out of the Jesus narrative of service that upends the typical human understandings of the hierarchical nature of power (Hauerwas and Coles, 2008: 316; see also Hauerwas and Vanier, 2008). This fits in quite well with the pacifism exemplified by Gandhi, King, and Suu Kyi as well. Yet Hauerwas ties it directly to war in a way that those three may not, and in a way with which I am distinctly uncomfortable (Hauerwas and Vanier, 2008: 50). As I present Hauerwas' construction of war, the deeper problems I see in Hauerwas' theology will become more evident.

As much as L'Arche has created beautiful communities and has an intimate relationship with peace and pacifism —of action (witnessing) that addresses the injustices against the marginalized—I am still unconvinced that it has real bearing on *war*. It does address the politics of death—where advances in liberalism have brought us to a place where we have drawn boundaries on what constitutes valued human life (see also Elshtain and Cloyd, 1995). It addresses the injustices experienced by a marginalized community, just as Gandhi, King, and Suu Kyi have done in their own communities. But I fail to see its larger relationship with military and structural power imbalances in the world. Maybe if this were a communal response in failed states where the marginalized were embraced I could see this as an appropriate response. For now, however, I will continue to make this argument: yes, Hauerwas does understand hospitality and vulnerability, but he does not address the fact that power in the modern state confronts him with a paradox: it is both a curse and a blessing. In disassembling power, in creating his critiques of what the "world" is in opposition to what the church is, in defining his theology so over and against different theologies, Hauerwas replicates power that can lead to harmful suppositions. Although he has clarified and thus weakened his church-versus-world dualism, what remains is a duality based on the privilege of living within what he criticizes the most: a liberal, modern state.

Blind to the Horrors

In Hauerwasian theology, there are at least three dualities that hinder a better understanding of Christian approaches to war. These include (in brief as they will be expanded upon further in this section):

1. **Spiritual versus physical:** This is a false dichotomy inherited from Platonic thought that is pervasive in most Western theology. Many times, Hauerwas makes the claim that the physical realm is unimportant to Christians because God provides them with all they need. The implications of such statements are that physical needs (not wants) and sufferings are of little importance to Christians.

While this speaks beautifully to a Christian's need to rely upon God in *spiritual* matters, it is rather cruel to suggest this to those who are actually suffering from such afflictions.

2. **Church versus world:** As addressed above, Hauerwas makes a clear distinction between the church, as a community of Cross-centered believers, and the world, a place without God that is corrupted by power.

3. **Privilege versus nonprivilege:** This is more implicit than explicit, and it is an outcome of the first two dualities. Hauerwas poses a paradox: while aptly criticizing the structural violence of the modern state, he fails to recognize how he benefits from it. He may eloquently write about hospitality and vulnerability, but Hauerwas is also ignorant of or immune to the horrors of the world.

These dualities amount to an understanding of the functioning of Christians and the church that is deeply optimistic and that displays an ignorance about the horrors of the world. In order to make the third duality/paradox clear, I will rely upon Marilyn McCord Adams' book *Christ and Horrors* (2006).

According to Marilyn McCord Adams, the human condition generally and the Divine-human relationship specifically are nonoptimal (Adams, 2006: 29) and are related to horrors. "Horrors" are defined "as evils the participation in (the doing or suffering of) which constitutes *prima facie* reason to doubt whether the participant's life could (given their inclusion in it) have positive meaning for him/her on the whole" (Adams, 2006: 32).[8] Horrors are an outcome of three mismatches: between the human psyche and biology; between human nature and the material world, "in which the necessities in life and flourishing seem and are difficult of access and in short supply"; and the "enormous gap between Divine and human personal capacities" (Adams, 2006: 38). The middle mismatch is particularly political, as politics cannot happen in a solitary environment but is a social activity in which contention arises over the distribution of scarce resources.

While Hauerwas' writings demonstrate an awareness of the third mismatch, his writings are seemingly oblivious to the first two. Some may argue that this is not the scope of Hauerwas' narrative theology, but if he is going to write about injustices, witnessing, and nonviolence, it would seem obvious that he would need to address some of these.

Remembering that dualisms of any kind are inherently problematic, as they lead to valuing one side over the other, Hauerwas' dualisms clearly prioritize and polarize the spiritual/church against the physical/worldly. Without directly addressing Hauerwas, Adams' theology offers a more integrated alternative. Adams recognizes that a division between the physical and spiritual realm exists (it is dualistically nonoptimal), but that these are not as polarized as Hauerwas (and others) might depict them to be, because humans are embodied spirits: "God has created us radically vulnerable to horrors, by creating us as embodied persons, personal animals, enmattered spirits in a material world of real or apparent scarcity such as this" (Adams, 2006: 37). When Adams (2006) repeatedly acknowledges that humans are "social animals" (37, 66, 159, 195, 228), the inevitable corruptibility of human institutions (203, 228), and the scarcity of the material world to meet the needs of human being(s) (32–38, 66), this rings of Niebuhrian realism—where humans are more likely to be virtuous on their own than in groups based upon the anxiety present in the human condition. This is evident in certain circumstances. Generally, it is witnessed that human-made "social systems institutionalize invidious distinctions, enshrine tribalism, nationalism, racism, caste systems or class distinctions, sexism and homophobia" (Adams, 2006: 228). Both Niebuhr's and Hauerwas' understandings of power are reflected in such a statement. (While I feel inclined to argue that Adams is more optimistic about the human condition than Niebuhr, the facts that she writes about evil and that her book focuses upon *horrors* holds me back.) Her realism is an acknowledgment of human frustrations at being in nonoptimal relationships with God and the material world.

Yet in Hauerwas, one finds little acknowledgment that the nonoptimal relationship is actually a problem (horror). Romand Coles points this out as well by quoting a previous work of Hauerwas' (with Wells, 2004): "God gives his people everything they need to follow him." Coles rejoins, "Of course, what Christian could *not* believe this to be true?" (Hauerwas and Coles, 2008: 210–11).[9] God *does* provide us with everything we need *spiritually*, but I disagree that God provides all humans in the world with every *material* need (and by this I mean needs basic for survival and even for "flourishing"). This disparity between spiritual and material is part of the basis for the horrors—horrors that Adams does not abstract; she names them: torture, rape, nationalism, sexism, genocide, and political martyrdom, among others.

Hauerwas also abstracts the effects of war on a human population. When he reflects upon the conversation between the Niebuhr brothers about the invasion of China (discussed in chapter 1), he believes that the best Christian response is prayer (Hauerwas, 1983: 136–38). This prompted me to liken such action as standing in a corner while a Burmese monk is being beaten by the Myanmar junta. Two decades later, Hauerwas argues that the question, "Should war be eliminated?" is a misnomer "because war has been eliminated for those who participate in God's history" (Hauerwas, Berkmann, and Cartwright, 2001: 423–24). Bluntly, this is nonsense for those, Christian or not, living in the midst of war. Their present suffering does matter. Furthermore, Hauerwas distorts and abstracts what war is and why it breaks out by blaming it solely on the need for "alleged democracies" to "run on speed, necessitating technologies designed to help us become the sort of people who do not need anyone" (Hauerwas and Vanier, 2008: 50–51). First, this fails to recognize that most wars today do not happen between the technologically advanced democracies; they happen in beleaguered states in the Global South. Second, it makes war a purposeful function of the state (à la political realism) and, as in most cases, not a result of weak political and economic systems. While he may counter that if we all lived according to the narrative, peace would exist, we live in a world where there are massive discrepancies (mismatches) in wealth, access, and power. Such an abstraction denies this and the need for Christians to witness and make peace in ways that directly challenge the duality of church versus world and the reasons war happen.

Adams' and Hauerwas' Christologies are in constant tension, as evidenced in the first dualism and now in the second, the church versus the world. On the one hand, for Hauerwas, the transcendent power of God allows Christians to wait on the Lord in patience toward injustices and sufferings. On the other hand, Adams may acknowledge that political theology has allowed itself to be constrained by the systemic and structural limitations of the material world (Adams, 2006: 206),[10] but this does not mean that action on the part of humans is completely unnecessary. In fact, political implications are laced throughout her book as she delineates how we, enabled through Christ, overcome horror. Thus, a resolution of the tension lies at the heart of Adams own argument: the transcendent metaphysical goodness of God. This metaphysic grants us an alternative to the church's withdrawal for the world.

Hauerwas' formulations of witness and peacemaking lead to a distinct duality between the church and the world—even though there is significant ambiguity in his work.[11] Witnessing and peacemaking are meant to overcome this division. Even within this desire to reconcile the two, the prioritizing of the church is still present: "The world cannot be the church, for the world, while still God's good creation, is a realm that knows not God and is thus characterized by the fears that constantly fuel the fires of violence" (Hauerwas, 1981: 109). While claiming the world as God's creation, Hauerwas makes the world (completely) oblivious to all good (God) and responsible for all violence a fait accompli. Although Hauerwas claims that it "is never a question of church or world. Rather it is a question of having a people so captured by the worship of God that that they can be for the world what the world so desperately needs" (Hauerwas and Coles, 2008: 111–12). Statements such as these do not hold the church accountable for any amount of injustice in the world or any justice that non-Cross-centered action may bring. The world is responsible for all bad and the church all good. Further, Hauerwas fears that the church has made too many accommodations to the world and has lost its countercultural edge (Hauerwas, 2001: 216). This makes it much easier for Christians to feel settled in their positions and more resistant to the world.

Hauerwas accurately describes the violence, the fear, and the pride that exist in the world—but has he not just negated God's power and love for the world by (1) saying that there is such a sharp distinction between church and world and (2) implicitly declaring that such corruptions do not exist in the church? When Hauerwas narrowly defines the church as a community of believers, he values—and implies that God values—believers over nonbelievers. Hauerwas argues for this structure using the "ethic of Jesus," his idea that by modeling and following the known reality of Jesus' life, the church knows how to act. This brings up a second issue, that the church is meant to be distinctly apolitical or anti-political. Adams would not be willing to leave it at this. Her Christology focuses on both the life (relationships and ministry) *and* sacrifice/resurrection of Jesus. Via this additional, significant element, of the *resurrection* of Christ, which is of lesser importance to Hauerwas' theology,[12] Adams' Christology holds deep implications for this world. The resurrection is crucial in understanding Adams' dependence upon embodiment. As will be clarified in the next section, all people in the world become the church, and all people become part of the mission of the church.

A continuation of Hauerwas' critique of the world is his problem with modern democracies. According to him, a liberal state is unequivocally based upon violence, and classic liberals "assume such violence can be 'redeemed by the progressive elimination of political exclusions'" (Hauerwas and Coles, 2008: 6). The provision of liberty and rights (elimination of political exclusions) is the violent heart of liberalism. This is related to the development and functioning of the modern state and its monopoly on violence (Westphalia):

> [T]he state becomes the sole protector of individual liberties: abstracting the right to kill from domestic politics, denying to any agents other than states the right to kill at home and abroad. The right to kill is the right to behave in violent ways toward other people—especially toward citizens of foreign states at war, and toward the uncivilized, whose very existence is a threat to civilized order. In recent circumstances, killing others is necessary, so it seems, for the security it provides (Hauerwas and Coles, 2008: 6).

States, created and maintained by the monopoly on violence, generate fear as a means of justifying their ends of space and power; this is the "politics of death" (Hauerwas and Coles, 2008: 7).[13] Those who subscribe to modernity and liberalism (like Niebuhr) have become be-holden to the idea that humans can control their destinies and manipu-late power (Hauerwas, 2001: 32–40).[14] The manner in which Niebuhr attempted to make his theology relevant to the liberal social order (or vice-versa) is seen by Hauerwas as a Constantinian attempt (Hauerwas, 2001: 220–24).

The conversation Hauerwas and Coles have in their book proposes an alternative to fear- and destruction-based politics "that cares for the commonalities, differences, and emergent irregularities of life" (Hau-erwas and Coles, 2008: 7). Any conception of "politics, justice, and democracy" has to hold the Cross at the center (Hauerwas and Coles, 2008: 105). While this is fundamentally a vision of democracy that does not apparently fully compromise Hauerwas' idea of Christianity (a beautiful, hospitable vision),[15] there is no suggestion of how such communities are going to work without the protection of the state. Hauerwas' problem is with liberalism rather than democracy (and one wonders where and how he is making the distinction), and with a state's power rather than its government. Nonetheless he fails to account for how these communities are going to exist without the operation of power. Communities and community activists can exist only as long as they are free from external threats. How does this happen without the state's monopoly on violence both internally and externally?

Hauerwas captures the problem of both physical and structural violence. For better or for worse, states depend on power to operate. Actual violence is the physical use of violence to uphold or change the system. The term "structural violence" indicates nonphysical power that creates a form of coercion that bends people to the status quo (see Galtung, 1969). For Hauerwas, the problem is how power is used to maintain a system of governance. Liberal democracies practice the politics of death, and the ability to govern in these states is directly related to how much (coercive) power is used to drive the system. How-ever, no system of government is perfect, including modern democracy. Yet liberal democracies may be praised for the privileges that they af-ford their citizens; there is a reason why those who monitor conflict, human development, and human rights typically include democratic measurements in their evaluations.[16] Still, Hauerwas rightly argues that liberal democracies also have within them systemic problems that exclude, marginalize, and harm (social injustices).

And what Hauerwas (along with Coles and Vanier) propose as a solution—a set of community oriented activities that demands the respect and recognition of all members of society—is one of the better ways to address structural violence. Those that witness are naming the violence, calling out the government to address it, and working individually to make things better—they are addressing the matters that matter. Yet Hauerwas, for all of the problems he has with liberalism as an internal form of government, does not recognize (1) that this is a better form of government than many people in the world have access to, (2) that the examples he gives as good operate best in a liberal democracy (at least at this point in history), and (3) that he gives no examples of how to address injustices in other places in the world. Thus, he has created a dualism that fails to recognize privilege and nonprivilege.

For instance, Coles especially emphasizes the early leadership of the Student Nonviolent Coordinating Committee (SNCC) in the U.S. South as an example of community activism. The SNCC leadership did experience hatred and violence that for a long while was not addressed by the power of the local or national government. What eventually put an end to the violence (but not racism) was the intervention of the state: President John F. Kennedy and Attorney General Robert F. Kennedy used the judicial system to support civil rights, and President Lyndon Johnson federalized the Alabama National Guard to support desegregation as well as signed into effect the Civil Rights Act of 1964. Herein lies the paradox: Hauerwas dislikes the entity that allows him to freely write and practice his religion as he sees fit (fortunately for him he neither sacrifices animals nor practices polygamy)—a liberal democratic state.

Hauerwas is privileged to write, speak, and teach what he wants to. He can be a community organizer or not. Ella Baker, Bob Moses, and Jean Vanier also had choices. Hauerwas says that should it come to it, he would be a willing martyr for Christ. Hopefully all Christians would be. But the fundamental truth remains: unless something radical changes in the United States, Hauerwas will never have to be a martyr. He is privileged to live in a society that protects his freedom. Even if I agree that this freedom is based off of both actual and structural violence, Hauerwas does not account for what it does provide.

The Hospitality of Timely Proactivity

The resolution to the tension between Hauerwas and Adams is hospitality. The church to Hauerwas is the community of Cross-centered believers. Hauerwas' church, narrowly defined, has all the time in the world to act toward injustices with patience; time is on its side, for speed is associated with war, modernity, and human control. Hauerwas does not convincingly make an urgent response to the horror of war, even though he makes a compelling argument demonstrating the vulnerability of hospitality.

A basic definition of politics is the fight for scarce resources or the distribution of power. Hauerwas' definition is the antidefinition: "politics . . . [are] the practices required for the formation of people in the virtues" necessary for the common good (Hauerwas and Coles, 2008: 112). At the heart of the Hauerwasian political ideal is vulnerability, and it functions by the practice of hospitality—an open embrace of people. Hauerwas claims that his "basic political conviction . . . is that people matter" (Hauerwas and Coles, 2008: 112). Hospitality requires learning from strangers (God is the ultimate stranger), which is another echo of Derrida's use of *The Sophist*. Nonviolence is slow and "wildly" patient work. Hospitality is slow, patient work; it is gentleness (Hauerwas and Coles, 2001: 26, 203; Hauerwas and Vanier, 2008). In short, Hauerwas' vision of hospitality is beautiful. Forgive me, but I do not trust it. I do not trust that it will be extended to all who need it because there are too many barriers that exist within the dualities presented in his work. There is not enough emphasis on a truly timely, proactive response to injustices in *the world* because of how much he values and draws exclusionary boundaries around *the church*.

Adams provides a solution. In various ways, she provides a concrete way for the church to witness horrors and not just turn away (withdrawal). By defining the "universal" church as *all humans* and by placing the church within such a deep and immense metaphysic, she demonstrates how the *realities* (horrors) of this world are relevant and disturbing to *God*. By acknowledging that God loves material creation (the world) (Adams, 2006: 39, 45, 49, 191, 216, 219, 226) and is attendant and aware enough of the horrors to send the Word to participate in, move against (Adams, 2006: 72), and suffer from said horrors (Adams, 2006: 35, 45, 51–52, 71, 108, 189), makes demands upon *us* to be equally attendant and aware of these horrors. We then operate on behalf of others before ourselves, and in some measure overcome the complicity that is wrought simply by living in this world, to whatever extent we experience any form of privilege. Why would we, as obedient Christians/children of God, abnegate responsibility toward material creation, whether that be environmental stewardship or care for other humans, no matter where they are?

It is clear that Adams sees operating on behalf of others in a political manner. She argues that Christ's own "ministry of preaching and teaching, of healing (of horror-reversal) and solidarity (sharing the horrors)" creates the "primary functions of the Church": "*testimony* and *solidarity*" (Adams, 2006: 202, emphasis in source). So far, this is very Hauerwasian (as is the statement "human efforts to change the system often do not so much eliminate as relocate horrors" [Adams, 2006: 202–3]). However, she takes it a step further than Hauerwas might (he may argue along these lines, but in a deeply ambiguous way) by arguing that "horror-participants come alongside other horror-participants to bear witness to the reality of the problem" and that actively witnessing and/or engaging in horror-defeat (to triumph over or recover from a horror) leads to a more intimate relationship with God. Further, part of the church, the missionary church, is meant to publicly "protest horror-perpetrating individuals and institutional structures, to demand and work for changes in personnel and institutions that will bring horrors to a stop" (Adams, 2006: 202). This also seems an unlikely Hauerwasian stance as it is slightly reminiscent of Constantinianism.

Additionally, simply by being born and living in a world of material scarcity, all humans become complicit with horror—more so when we "live in societies that defend their interests by warfare and so accept horror-perpetration as a chosen means to or a side effect of its military aims" (Adams, 2006: 36). Hauerwas addresses this in his critique of the modern state, but he misses it when he fails to engage problems outside the (his) modern, democratic state. Equally, redemptively, just as humans are complicit with horrors, so is Jesus by virtue of being a subject of the Roman Empire. Yet Jesus also spoke out against marginalization and injustices; he spoke against complicity (as does Hauerwas) (Adams, 2006: 72). But this leads to another divergence between Hauerwas and Adams. Where Hauerwas would not necessarily call for such direct action, Adams makes it clear that acting against complicity demands something of the "church universal"—the entire human race (Adams, 2006: 201). And in the face of such a grand scheme of salvation/horror-defeat/reconciliation with God (the metaphysic), this makes our inactivity toward the horrors of the world even more selfish and cowardly.

This means that the church operates in the world, and it recognizes that all forms of the church and all people in the world are part of the power structure. We are all complicit; we all participate in and suffer from horrors. By sending his Son, God provides us with the means to defeat horror. But for Adams this does not absolve us of responsibility to address horrors in this world. This is what a church-withdrawal-from-world dualism ignores as it leads to the privilege-versus-nonprivilege modern state paradox. We do not get to claim some kind of sacred-non-action place by being in "The Church" while living in a country paid for by warfare and physical, social, and economic inequalities. Such benefits are neither apolitical nor free of burden (lacking in complicity). If anything, Christians bear a greater burden.

Moving Beyond

Such a burden can be assumed by practicing hospitality. For Hauerwas, hospitality is patient witnessing and peacemaking. But this hospitality needs to engage the world, not stand outside of it for whatever reason. And while Hauerwas will see my theology as compromised,

Christians can use hospitality as a means of addressing the horrors—as a more directly political means of peacemaking. This form of peacemaking also has to recognize that time is of the essence because caring for people means caring for their physical and spiritual well-being. For people with access to the trappings of privilege, it means recognizing when others are in harm's way, recognizing their vulnerability.

Niebuhr's Christian realism grants an understanding of power, but it is an understanding that needs to be tempered with the recognition of all people's vulnerability. Hauerwasian pacifism grants such vulnerability, but at a cost. The cost is an abnegation of responsibility for the safety and precarity of the lives of others. While he can make a decision about the precarity of his own life, Hauerwas cannot make this decision for other people, especially when they are already constrained and oppressed by structural violence(s). Such an imposition is distinctly irresponsible.

The question remains: How can power and vulnerability come together in a way that accepts responsibility for others (hospitality)? Previous chapters illustrated that taking responsibility for others in international relations must involve some amount of power. But the overarching argument of the book must also allow that untempered power creates massive amounts of harm as either imperialism or misguided best efforts. A better answer is situated within the Just War tradition, specifically within *jus ad bellum* as proactive last resort.

CHAPTER SIX

The Offer of Hospitality

Just War is at a new crossroads, where those who are addressing contemporary problems and updating definitions and applications are departing from those who adhere to traditional ones. Such a departure helps ground this book's argument to "weaken" last resort by lengthening the temporal process of *jus ad bellum* in order to provide a way to prevent the outbreak of conflict in failed states. Mindful of the fear and resentment of imperialism, this action is meant to provide better security for all and proactively help those on the margins of international affairs. Activity, whether it is aid, foreign direct investment, or military support, must be grounded in good boundaries with respect for sovereignty (even if it is challenged) and the true *needs* of those being helped: hospitality.

It is argued that Just War thinking is a tradition. Unlike a theory, it changes and adapts to new situations (Rengger, 2002). In the West, the development of the Just War tradition is closely related to the development of the modern state system. Thus, the type of wars the tradition has focused upon have been interstate wars, the kind of wars that have dramatically decreased in number since World War II. In the contemporary arena, the majority of wars happen in failed states, with devastating methods (child soldiers, high civilian death, and maiming and rape as strategies) in seemingly never-ending conflicts (Gettleman, 2010). Even though scholarship to contemporize Just War has been done (see Heinze and Steel, 2009; Johnson, 1999), current research needs to find a way to address some of the most pressing issues of contemporary global politics while staying focused on the tradition's purpose: to be an ethical constraint on the path to war and during war itself.

The eternal tension between realism and liberal idealism, as noted over time in the writings of Thucydides, Augustine, Kant, Machiavelli, and others, is echoed in the tension between Niebuhr's Christian realism and Hauerwas' contemporary Christian pacifism. It is the tension between claiming power for a greater good and shunning it for another interpretation of the greater good. Combining Just War with hospitality brings these two traditions together—probably in ways with which neither is going to be entirely comfortable.[1] This study will not apologize for any discomfort. States must provide for the security of their interests, whether the interests pertain to citizens, borders, or in the global system—but not at the expense of others, which political realism allows. Instead, a proactive seeking of security means seeking security for more people than those within a state's borders; it means securing peace and life for those outside of the state as well. In the end, this will provide for *all* people's security.

Hospitality enables this. Traditional understandings of hospitality constrain it to actions *within* the state. Jacques Derrida's use of the conversation between Xenos and Thaetetus highlights that Xenos is arriving in Thaetetus' state. The sovereign locale, the state, is the site of hospitality—as the place and authority that can offer it (Derrida and Dufourmantelle, 2005: 5–9). This chapter will argue, instead, that every international actor—states, IGOs, NGOs, multinational corporations, citizens—must push hospitality outside of the state as well, in a way that is not unfamiliar to the Ancient Greek setting of *The Sophist* nor to Christian practices of hospitality. However, the tension that must be addressed is one that Derrida also noted: hospitality is conditioned by the eternal tension between raison d'état and ethics (Derrida and Dufourmantelle, 2005: 73). The last resort criterion has been conditioned by this tension as well, and changing notions of sovereignty help resolve it.

Just War at a Crossroads

Just War is a "fragmented" conversation "comprising many different sub-traditions, and indeed sub-sub-traditions" and is, therefore, "only a 'theory' in the very loosest sense" (Bellamy, 2005: 3; see also May, 2007: 4).[2] Material on the tradition has proliferated in the past few years, and it is being drawn into contemporary debates about issues such as nuclear weapons (Royden, 2014; O'Brien, 1992; Zaw, 1991), private military companies (Eckert, 2009), humanitarian intervention (Chesterman, 2002; ICISS, 2001; Johnson, 1999; Walzer, 1977), robotic warfare (Singer, 2009), feminism and gender (Poe, 2008; Sjoberg, 2006), and legitimate authority (sovereignty) (Denike, 2008). All of the publications cited speak to the tradition's malleability in relation to current events. Further publications approach the issue of the divergence of the tradition into old and new schools. Nicholas Fotion argues that there are those who "rigidly" adhere to traditional interpretations of Just War and those who are trying to contemporize (loosen) it to deal with new problems, such as insurgency (Fotion, 2007: 155).

Unlike the Christian approaches to war discussed in the previous two chapters, the Just War tradition does not have one contemporary Christian voice that holds the same attention as Niebuhr for Christian realism or Hauerwas for Christian pacifism. From the ancient and medieval thought of Augustine, Thomas Aquinas, Francisco de Vitoria, and Alberico Gentili to the modern Catholic bishops, George Weigel, James Turner Johnson, Paul Ramsey, and Jean Bethke Elshtain, there is a multitude of Christian scholars who contribute to the tradition. However, it must be made clear that as much as the Just War tradition has been greatly informed and nurtured by Christian voices, typically Catholic, it is no longer a single-faith domain. Many voices contribute to the conversation; the tradition is informed by "Catholic canon law and theology, Protestant religious thought, secular philosophy, international law, military theory and practice, and the experience of statecraft" (Johnson, 2005).

Still, most of the Christian scholars base theological justifications for war on *agape*, because God's expectations for Christians to care for others is intrinsic to *agape* (Johnson, 1999: 111). From Augustine to modern scholars, such as Paul Ramsey and James Turner Johnson, those who see the connection between *agape* and Just War believe the tradition and its practices to be a product of Christian discipleship. In particular, Johnson, who has been joined in more recent years by Daniel M. Bell Jr., writes eloquently about the contemplation and intentionality involved, on the part of the Christian, in the making and fighting of war (see Johnson, 1981: xxx–xxxiii; 1999: 5; and Bell, 2009). In contrast to this, Jean Bethke Elshtain, who also grounds her work on Just War in *agape*, seems to miss the virtues of discipline and discipleship. Instead, her work on Just War creates a power-over discourse that is in contrast to most understandings of how *agape* should be performed. This forces me to address Jean Bethke Elshtain's *Just War against Terror* (2004).

Political Manipulations: Last Resort Over Time

There are three pieces to Just War thinking: *jus ad bellum*, the justice of starting a war; *jus in bello*, just conduct within a war; and *jus post bellum*, justice after a war. As I am particularly concerned with last resort, a criterion of *jus ad bellum*, I am far less concerned with *jus in bello* and *jus post bellum* here. Further, there is a plethora of research and conversation on what exactly *jus in bello* entails and a growing literature on *jus post bellum* that this chapter does not need to elaborate upon. Instead, discussion will stay centered on the qualifying criteria of *jus ad bellum*, which are:

- just cause (typically self-defense or defense of another state),
- legitimate authority (a state),
- right intent (peace),
- proportionality (does the response fit the cause?),

- last resort (have all other measures been exhausted?), and
- reasonable chance of success (see May, 2008; Bellamy, 2005, 2009; Charles, 2005; Johnson, 1999; U.S. Catholic Bishops, 1983: 18–20; and Walzer, 1977).

Like the other criteria of *jus ad bellum*, last resort acts as a constraint on the motivation to go to war. Simply stated, a just war may be entered into when all, or enough, of the criteria have been met (see Bell, 2009: 94–95). To satisfy the last resort criterion, all parties must be able to prove that all diplomatic and nonmilitary alternatives have been exhausted and are known to be unsuccessful (Bell, 2009: 185; Wester, 2007: 60; Elshtain, 2004: 61; ICISS, 2001: 36; Childress, 1982: 75). In last resort, there are two standards to be met. First, the reasonableness standard is met when the pacific (negotiation or adjudication) or coercive (economic sanctions or blockades) measures

- have been created appropriately by including all parties;
- have been completed in a timely manner, either by recognizing when war-delaying measures are doing more harm than good or by *giving up hope that peace will emerge* (this is a key piece of my later argument);
- have been carried out fairly and with stability; and
- have followed proper procedural standards (Lango, 2006: 2–7; ICISS, 2001: 36).

Second, these measures must meet the awfulness standard. Awfulness depends upon the feasibility of such measures. (Are they realistic in relation to other available options?) More importantly, it evaluates whether these alternative measures are truly less harmful than going to war (Wester, 2007: 66–67; Lango, 2006; Childress, 1982: 75). Overall, these measures—such as negotiations, adjudication, blockades, sanctions, and embargoes—come too late or are far too harmful to failed states.[3]

There are several factors that have hampered the utilization of last resort. The first—the strongest—is best articulated by Michael Walzer, who argues that there could always be one more option before declaring war. This would prolong the injustice and instability already happening, making the situation far more unjust than if war were more immediately entered into. He argues that of course "measures short of war are preferable to war itself" if they hold the promise of an effectiveness equal or similar to the war (Walzer, 1977: 85). But these measures cannot be tried indefinitely. Fotion adds that if last resort is "taken literally, last resort is meaningless"—there will always be another option yet to try. Thus, in his lengthy discussion of last resort, Fotion argues it should be better known as "last reasonable resort" (2007: 14–15). His forward-thinking work on last resort will be drawn upon in the last part of this chapter.

The second factor relates to the constant tension between the interrelated criteria of legitimate authority and last resort (see Bell, 2009: 187; 2006: 350; Bergoffen, 2008: 74); it is the same tension as that between realism and idealism—that is, the importance of state power and the ethical constraints on state behavior, such as international law and norms. For instance, is war "absolute" (à la Carl von Clausewitz),[4] or should states constrain their power? Writing as a morally, normatively constrained Christian, Augustine still created an early conceptualization of raison d'état that resides in the ability of the *righteous* sovereign (legitimate authority) to do whatever s/he discerns to be righteous (taking for granted that what is presumed to be righteous will always be the best for everyone) (Augustine, 1996: 41–42, 163–65, 170). Aquinas took this further by placing authority within the Catholic Church, which was the source of most, if not all, political power during his time period (see *Summa Theologica,* Secunda Secundae, Question 1, Article 10).

Therefore, the advent of the crisis of authority during the pre-Enlightenment period, especially as it led to the Reformation, shifted many Just War fundamentals. Since philosophers and theologians could no longer count on knowing for certain that a particular side in a war had God's blessing, they had to assume that both sides might actually have it (Bellamy, 2008: 53). This meant the focus in the Just War tradition shifted from *jus ad bellum* to *jus in bello.* Sovereign power and the separation of church and state were further expounded upon in the 1648 Peace of Westphalia. At this point, sovereigns were almost unquestioningly understood to have just cause as a means of protecting the state. It was the complication of legitimate authority that led to a more developed last resort, especially as it relates to the tension between raison d'état and ethical constraints (for a lengthier discussion on this see Johnson, 2005).

Protorealist writings of Machiavelli introduce and strengthen raison d'état; since life was a constant quest for survival, human history, then, was a constant cycle of civil strife. Not only could the state channel this energy into good, the state provided for security against strife. Thus, what was good for the state was good for humankind, and the state had to have the freedom to act: raison d'état (Bellamy, 2008: 56–57). This realist/realpolitik thinking was then further developed by Thomas Hobbes and Clausewitz,[5] and formalized by Niebuhr, Morgenthau, and Waltz. Political realism's valuation of state power and self-interest purposely leads to a sense of constraint via rationality and capability as seen in the balance of power. However, individual conceptualizations of morality or ethical obligations have little value in international affairs.[6] Realpolitik's emphasis upon self-interest and sovereign authority is all that is needed to declare war; in other words, "states . . . always have a right to fight" (Walzer, 1977: 63; see also Bellamy, 2008: 76). The development of raison d'état compromises the need to determine last resort.

In contrast to scholars who advocate raison d'état and realpolitik, other scholars believe that a war is not made just simply because a sovereign wants it. This rejection of absolute sovereign authority and raison d'état prompted the rationalization for last resort procedures, such as Gentili's suggestion of arbitration as an alternative to war (Bellamy, 2008: 53–61). Later, while Clausewitzian ideas of absolute warfare were gaining ground in the 1800s, last resort was becoming codified in international law. In 1907, the second Hague conference attempted to establish a system of obligatory arbitration. The "most significant innovation" to *jus ad bellum* since Vitoria and Gentili was advanced in the League of Nations, where states were required to "justify their decision to wage wars to their peers, who would in turn choose whether or not to accept those justifications" (Bellamy, 2008: 102). Currently, something similar is required by the United Nations; states still face a form of arbitration/discernment by having to "persuade their peers of the legitimacy of the case for war" (Bellamy, 2008: 114; see also Walzer, 1977: 78–79).

Even in contemporary international politics, both pacific and coercive measures already occur in a warlike arena (see Bell, 2009: 188–90). Coercive economic measures like sanctions and embargoes can be seen as acts of war for all of the damage they do to the populations of the target states—for instance, the Oil-for-Food program in Iraq (see Andreas, 2005; Naylor, 2001; and Nossal, 1989).[7] Even pacific measures like going to the United Nations for adjudication can be a signaling of intent. An example of this is U.S. Secretary of State Colin Powell's 2003 address to the General Assembly regarding weapons of mass destruction in Iraq. It is not that these measures are unsuccessful and without their place in international affairs—they work to varying degrees of success in different situations, such as embargoes on South Africa's Apartheid state. But these measures do need to be seen as acts of hostility, if not war, and not measures that define a prewar threshold to be met, such as last resort.

Contemporary and historic understandings of last resort have both amounted more to posturing than to measures for preventing war (see Bell, 2009: 188–90). Neither pacific measures nor coercive measures create or maintain a true peace, and because of this may enact structural violence that may not be any less damaging than a full-scale military intervention. At the temporal point under discussion, chance of war is already high and structural violence is already likely in place. These measures are reminiscent of Roman fetial law. In order to declare war, the Roman Senate first sent emissaries with its demands, which were often "non-negotiable and . . . set at unacceptable levels," to enemy states and then waited thirty-three days for a reply. If the enemy state did not comply, then the religious leaders, the *fetiales*, deliberated the justice of the war. Thus, the proposed adjudication or negotiation by Rome was more of a warning to the enemy state than an actual effort toward promoting peace (Bellamy, 2008: 19). This signaling is how last resort has functioned. I propose that last resort be retooled to become a proactive *jus ad bellum* criterion, a true means of staving off war. This proposal requires one to recognize the undeniable shift in the nature of war and to reconceptualize what it means to be secure.

The Ethic of Responsibility: Elshtain, Just War, and American Exceptionalism

While most writings on hospitality and international relations are by postmodernists, hospitality is intrinsically related to Christian conceptions of *agape*—which is fundamental to addressing vulnerability. *Agape* informs hospitality's call to care for others; it is also a historical basis for the Christian justification for war (Bell, 2009; Augustine, 1996: 8, 32; Ramsey, 1992: 14, 17; 1954: 120–21; Langan, 1991: 172; Deane 1963: 164). And this is paramount to overcoming the power differential inherent in the dualities involving an in-group that is valued above or at the expense of an out-group. Having in-groups that are valued for their perceived legitimacy constructs an inherent power dynamic that is problematic for gender relations, identity politics, and international relations alike because this dualism subjugates and subordinates. It detracts from human security and tends to stay focused on state sovereignty and power as the matters that constitute international relations.

Politically, it may be simple to describe vulnerable populations in reference to self/citizen versus other/foreigner (Baker, 2009: 98). Citizenship affirms the actuality of belonging by birth or oath (Baker, 2009: 101). In terms of security, the enemy or oppositional group is the other, and this connotation then tacitly acknowledges the vulnerability both sides feel in the presence of each other (Thaetetus and Xenos again). The embrace of hospitality does indeed make the person, collectivity, or state vulnerable, but, again, vulnerability does not invite abuse. Thus, while the collectivity or state becomes or is in the process of becoming vulnerable, how does it practice *agape*?

Agape: Discipline in the Just War Tradition

James Turner Johnson argues, in essence, that Christianity's reluctance to engage in war—a reluctance that informs the restraint of the Just War tradition—stems from Christianity's own past with vulnerability. Since Christianity began as a persecuted subaltern identity with no access to power, the belief system largely identified with pacifism. Christianity's accrual of power means that believers now have to grapple with the best practices of power. Furthermore, Christians can never be sure that they have the absolute right or the approval of God to practice violence. Therefore, "Christians who have taken up the sword [should remember] that they can never act as though what they do is absolutely right. The Christian warrior must feel a hand on his shoulder and a cautioning voice in his ear, even though he believes he is right to have taken up arms" (Johnson, 1981: xxxi). The discipline it takes to properly practice the Just War tradition is rooted in Christian virtues. Thus, Johnson's own writings on the tradition and when to engage in war reflect this discipline—his work is cautious, nuanced, and understated.

This is reflected in his book on humanitarian intervention from 1999, *Morality and Contemporary Warfare*. Throughout his many publications, Johnson has always balanced the moral requirements of the Just War tradition against the power maneuvers of political realism (see Johnson, 2011, 1999, 1981). Once again acknowledging that no one can claim absolute certainty in the going to and fighting of war, Johnson navigates the difficult sovereignty issues implicit in humanitarian interventions. He makes two important claims in his reflections, ones that are important to illustrating how inharmonious Elshtain's claims in *Just War against Terror* are. The first claim is that because we cannot be sure of a war's righteousness, we must treat our precarious enemies with care. The "worst features" of "contemporary warfare" include:

> the understanding of war as an all-or-nothing conflict that can end only when one side is entirely victorious and the other entirely vanquished or driven into unconditional submission; the

conception of the enemy as including all members of the opposing society, making a distinction between combatants and noncombatants irrelevant; the use of atrocity as a means of war; the use of ethnic, religious, or other cultural differences in much the same way as ideology was earlier employed to make the enemy appear less than fully human and, in any case, totally in the wrong (Johnson, 1999: 5).

The second claim is that an obligation to care for neighbors based upon *agape* exists within the Just War tradition (Johnson, 1999: 111). Johnson does complicate this obligation, especially in light of intervention, because it is difficult to ascertain which obligation in international affairs a state is required to adhere to the most—obligations to the Westphalian system, to political communities which may help end the conflict, or to the victims of conflicts (1999: 102–3). Both of these claims illustrate the discipline that exists within Johnson's work, a discipline based in *agapic* thought that creates normative constraints on war (which also conditions Johnson's discourse as one of thoughtful and quiet contemplation).

Like Johnson, Daniel M. Bell Jr., one of the emerging theological voices on the Just War tradition, finds that Christian discipline and virtuosity are the only practices that will keep the tradition viable (Bell, 2009, 2007, 2006). The use of Just War thinking today is split between policy makers who often use it as a prescriptive tool for maintaining the power of the state and Christians who practice it as a virtue ethics approach to war. For Bell, the virtue ethics approach is a difficult road to follow, as it severely limits the wars that may be entered into and the methods for fighting the war (see Bell, 2009: 90–95). This rationale is often reminiscent of Hauerwas: the Christian discipline of Just War "is at home in the church [as opposed to the state] and as a consequence faithfulness, not survival, is the principal concern" (Bell, 2009: 201). This grants Christian warriors the knowledge that the violence they are participating in is not the final justice and alleviates "the temptation to step outside of the discipline in order to thwart defeat" (Bell, 2009: 201).

Further, this discipline informs how Christians are to think about their enemies: with love for the other. Just War as a Christian discipline practiced and informed by the church is a loving act in three ways, according to Bell. Just War is an "alien act of love" because it (1) limits the way war is fought, (2) curtails the duration of war, and (3) echoing Augustine, fights for the good of the enemy (Bell, 2009: 176–77). While some of Bell's conclusions are a bit naïve,[8] his intentionality in grounding the Just War tradition in the practices of virtue is powerful and stands in sharp contrast to Elshtain's most recent work on the tradition.

Elshtain's Inhospitable *Agape*

Because her work has garnered so much attention and is lacking in the contemplation and discipline of Johnson and Bell's work,[9] Jean Bethke Elshtain's *Just War against Terror* lends itself to criticisms. Before deconstructing the complicit and hegemonic thinking in *Just War against Terror*, it is important to place it alongside her well-regarded contributions to international relations. It is said that every one of Elshtain's thoughts are worthy of publication, and one can conclude by looking at her curriculum vitae that they are. Beginning in the late 1970s, Elshtain mainly focused on political theory from a feminist perspective. As highlighted in chapter 1, she first challenged the gendered divisions of the public and private spheres (1981) before tackling war as a deeply gendered subject that constructs citizenship through participation in war (1987). Elshtain is also a theologian, and although she was raised and remains a Protestant, she is greatly influenced by Catholic theology. After *Women and War* (1987), Elshtain published quite prolifically on Just War, using the tradition as a way of speaking out against injustices in the world. To better understand her ethos, it is helpful to pause on one of her strongest, even if smallest, theologies: *Who Are We? Critical Reflections and Hopeful Possibilities* (2000).

As explained previously, in *Who Are We?* Elshtain argues that as embodied creatures created by the Creator, humans are called to be in relationship with other people. Before we can truly engage in our human relationships, we must be in relationship with God. In such a relationship, living in the *imago dei*, we are free (Elshtain, 2000: 18–19). This turns modern interpretations of freedom upside down and echoes Niebuhr's theology in *The Nature and Destiny of Man* (1964). It does not mean we are free to do whatever we like, whenever we like. To live without limits, *sicut deus*, means that we are unable to recognize God's sovereignty or our responsibility to others (Elshtain, 2000: 19). Freedom means we understand that we are finite beings called to live within the boundaries that God has established for us.

God calls us to communion (Elshtain, 2000: 28; see also Elshtain, 2008: 4, 203–6). Like hospitality, worship is a communal activity that establishes relationships between God and self, God and community, and between the community participants. In community and in freedom, we are responsible to each other: "Being free means 'being free for the other,' because the other has bound me to him" (Elshtain, 2000: 15). In such hospitable responsibility, Elshtain, in contrast to Hauerwas, exhorts that Christians are duty-bound to speak out in a world that is both good and also fallen (2000: 127–28). Christians live in hope and expectation, and we are then able to speak out against the destruction of creatures and creation alike (Elshtain, 2000: 154).

While Elshtain mainly focuses on domestic issues, such as abortion, her emphasis on "naming things accurately" is reflected in her deliberations in *Just War against Terror*. There is no denying that the Taliban was (and is reemerging as) a tyrannical government, yet it must be said that Elshtain is clearly naming the horrors of political violence *as she sees them*. For her, all the wrong in Afghanistan comes from a neo-orientalist vision of Islam and all of the justice from the United States' moral hegemony. This is elementary thinking, and this, as well as Elshtain's loaded discourse, weakens any worthy argument in the book, tarnishes Elshtain's scholarly reputation, and separates her from historical and contemporary theological understandings of the Just War tradition.

Just War against Terror (2004) reads as an unnuanced apologetic for her principal authorship of "What We're Fighting For: A Letter from America," issued on February 12, 2002 (see Elshtain, 2004: 193–218).

Written and signed by fifty-nine other American academics, the letter defends the war in Afghanistan as providing security for the United States, its citizens, and "American values," which include human dignity and equality, the legitimate role of government for the flourishing of civil society, and freedom (Elshtain, 2004: 74–75). According to her, 9/11 was a direct outcome of the threat posed by the Taliban regime to the rest of the world and the Afghan population.

The main argument of the book establishes why Afghanistan is a Just War, and the epilogue in the paperback edition justifies Iraq as well (Elshtain, 2004: 183). This defense of both as Just Wars is brief and cursory, playing into a growing fear that *jus ad bellum* has become a permissive "check-mark" worksheet instead of a deliberative process (see Bell, 2009: 77–80, 153, 239; Fotion, 2007: 25–33). In contrast to most of the book, which is an elegant contemplation of the tradition and its role in contemporary events, her deliberation upon Afghanistan and *jus ad bellum* criteria is short: only three pages (Elshtain, 2004: 115–17). While the rest of the chapter complicates both *jus ad bellum* and *jus in bello*, it is more of a general discussion than an examination of the war in Afghanistan or the War on Terror.

Perhaps even more problematic is the book's defensive and deeply anxious reaction to the events of 9/11. Elshtain discursively sets the American psyche apart as fragile and in need of a powerful (military), protective response. For instance, she writes:

> If we live from day to day in fear of deadly attack, the goods we cherish become elusive. Human beings are fragile creatures. We cannot reveal the fullness of our being, including our deep sociality, if airplanes are flying into buildings or snipers are shooting at us randomly or deadly spores are being sent through the mail (Elshtain, 2004: 47).

She is correct: human life is fragile. But is the human spirit? Elshtain references only the events and anxieties that immediately followed 9/11 in American public life. Yet if we cast back to the aftermath of World War I and World War II or contemplate the current peace, albeit fragile, that exists after the juntas in South America, South African Apartheid, the civil wars in Yugoslavia, or the Troubles in Northern Ireland, we witness the essential resilience and recuperative ability of the human spirit: a former Tupamaro,[10] José Mujica, leads Uruguay; Nelson Mandela became the first president of post-apartheid South Africa; and Queen Elizabeth II shook hands with former Irish Republican Army member Martin McGuinness, now deputy first minister of Northern Ireland.

While she claims her treatment of Islam and Muslims is neither essentialist nor determinist, it is. Much of *Just War against Terror* reads as a stridently neo-orientalist account that justifies, in moralistic terms, America's hegemonic mission to be a military force in the world. But it is a moralized military force against a particular population. Edward Said describes orientalism as a Western way of viewing the Middle East as a conquered territory filled with people who are less intelligent, incapable of being educated, and sexually deviant (2004: 61; 1985: 90–91; 1978: 7). More recently, it is understood that neo-orientalism is the extension of such insidious thinking to all people associated with Islam (Akram, 2000: 7).

Elshtain frames the idea that the War on Terror is a just war in religious-ideological terms: "They [Muslims] loathe us [Westerners/Americans] because of who we are and what our society represents" (2004: 3; see also 23). All good things—like Western liberal democratic values of (moral) equality, freedom, and separation of church and state—are related to Christianity (see Elshtain, 2004: 6, 26–45), and all bad things—like "appallingly low standards of education and literacy; the absence of political freedom, a human rights culture, and solid economic development, and the officially sanctioned second-place status of women" are related to Islam (Elshtain, 2004: 138). She uncritically accepts this neo-orientalist account of the aftermath in Bosnia:

"People victimized by genocide or abandoned by the international community do not make good neighbors, as their thirst for vengeance, their irredentism, and their acceptance of violence as a means of generating change can turn them into future threats. In Bosnia, where the United States and Europe maintained an arms embargo against the Muslims, extremist Islamic fighters and proselytizers eventually turned up to offer support. . . . The failed state of Bosnia became a haven for Islamic terrorists shunned elsewhere in the world" (Power, 2002, quoted in Elshtain, 2004: 169).

Elshtain's reliance on clash-of-civilizations discourse accepts a binary of a supposed global split between the West and Islam, with Muslims as barbarians at the gate of American hegemonic exceptionalism.

How Elshtain "accurately" names the problem of radical Islamic terrorism poses a significant problem. True, she attempts to define what terrorism is, but she does so without relying upon any of the recognized experts in the field, such as Paul Wilkinson, Bruce Hoffman, or Martha Crenshaw, nor does she recognize that the terms "terror," "terrorism," and "terrorist" are highly contested and deeply subjective (Elshtain, 2004: 18–20). Further, throughout *Just War against Terror* she connects the War on Terror only to a war on radical Islamists, rarely acknowledging that the ideologies that define terrorist organizations stem from both religious and secular sources. Nor does she acknowledge that then, as now, radical Islamist violence does not account for a majority of all of the substate political violence in the world (Europol, 2009: 11; Hoffman, 2006: 86). Most terrorism studies scholars would agree with her that terrorism targets noncombatants as opposed to states and so-called legitimate militaries. Yet this simplifies a complicated debate and fails to account for postcolonial political violence and state terrorism.[11] In sharp contrast, she valorizes the U.S. military establishment, claiming that "no institution in America pays more attention to ethical restraint on the use of force than does the U.S. military" (Elshtain, 2004: 67). While it is only fair to acknowledge that she wrote this before the establishment of Camps X-Ray and Delta in Guantanamo Bay and before the Abu Ghraib scandal broke (and she does quite clearly condemn the My Lai massacre [Elshtain 2004: 18]), it is not like the U.S. military establishment is completely innocent of other atrocities, such as rape (see Enloe, 2000, 1989).

Elshtain argues that there is a crisis within Islam itself, saying that the Muslim community was silent or refused to condemn Osama bin Laden after 9/11 (2004: 135–37). But in fact, on September 11, 2001, the Council on American-Islamic Relations (CAIR) released a statement signed by eleven Islamic organizations condemning the attacks (CAIR, 2001). And over the next few years, CAIR compiled a sixty-eight-page collection documenting the Muslim response after 9/11, which vilifies the attacks and the terrorists behind them (CAIR, 2007). She also claims that there are gender emancipatory voices in Islam, yet does not cite any of them. Instead, she relies upon Western voices (2004: 38–44), even though outstanding scholarly voices from Islam were available, like those of Leila Ahmed (1992) and Valentine Moghadam (2003).

Finally, in reference to Augustine, Elshtain introduces *agape* as an "ethic of responsibility" embedded within Just War thinking and proceeds to use it to argue for humanitarian intervention in Afghanistan (Elshtain, 2004: 57). The "obligation of loving one's neighbour," *agape*, means saving "the lives of others" via just wars (Elshtain, 2004: 57). Such a war (humanitarian intervention) would restore "human dignity" to people, specifically the Afghan people oppressed by the Taliban (Elshtain, 2004: 59–60). Others fear that this is an articulation of an American exceptionalism evocative of city-on-the-hill thinking that seems to name the United States as the sole power able to achieve and responsible for other states' salvations (O'Driscoll, 2007: 488–89). Cian O'Driscoll believes that this is a misconstrual of Augustine that grants permission to the United States to pursue favorable humanitarian interventions under the guise of justice (2007: 485, 489). (This echoes Chris Brown's argument that many humanitarian interventions have not happened without serving the intervening state's self interest [Brown, 2002: 136].)

This is a curious and ahistorical manipulation of *agape*. The Taliban was not a good government, and Afghan women were treated indescribably terribly. Al Qaeda is not an entity deserving of respect or legitimacy. Nevertheless, this does not excuse Elshtain's positioning of the hegemonic United States as the "Just Warrior" off to protect the

"Beautiful Soul" of Afghanistan (Elshtain, 1987).[12] *Just War against Terror* does not present the best way to love Afghanistan and Afghans. It is a presentation of the best way for the United States to apparently provide superior security in the face of an overconstructed, overblown terrorist threat (see Jackson, 2005). Paul Ramsey argues that Augustine's notion of *agape* is problematic because the one offering love seeks something (righteousness) from the object of love (Ramsey, 1954: 120–21).[13] Elshtain has adopted a similarly problematic interpretation of *agape* that serves the interest of the actor (the security of and alleviation of anxiety about terrorist threats in the United States) instead of the interests of the one being acted upon. Damningly, Nicholas Rengger argues that in *Just War against Terror* Elshtain has grasped at Sauron's "ring of power" (2004: 114–15).[14]

Still, it is Elshtain who rescues Elshtain. She is acting as a moral voice by attempting to name the problem in Afghanistan. In many regards, this is admirable, even though it is done in an offensively clumsy manner. Yet the aspiration to be a voice to the world threads itself throughout all of her work and culminates in her 2005 Gifford Lectures (Elshtain, 2008). Her greater ethos informs how she approaches a metaphysical and macrovision of sovereignty. Because humans are called into community and a responsibility to others (Elshtain, 2000, 2008), Elshtain conceives of sovereignty in a moral, ethical way.[15] If we take from *Sovereignty* (2008) the idea that sovereignty is representative of a loving relationship between God and creation, state and individual, then we can begin to construct an idea of sovereignty that can coexist and work with hospitality.[16] When sovereignty is strictly defined, hospitality becomes limited.

Hospitality as Performative *Agape*

Internationally, sovereignty prioritizes the laws, customs, and norms of both the state of origin and the state system itself (Elshtain, 2008: 5). The state's internal values establish how it interacts in global affairs, and the Westphalian system, bound by its own norms, will often reinforce this.[17] In effect, this keeps security as a primary obligation. There are two limits on hospitality stemming from raison d'état. First, hospitality cannot transcend a limit of its own making: "[I]f there is to be hospitality, then there must be a foreigner; and, for the foreigner to be appear foreign in the first place, there must exist hospitality of some kind" (Baker, 2009: 111). State-based sovereignty, which identifies distinct territories, governments, and people, automatically identifies host versus foreign states' territories, government, and people. Second, hospitality has an intrinsic power dynamic: the "laws of hospitality" are dependent upon "the familial despot, the father, the spouse, and the boss, the master of the house who lays down the laws of hospitality" (Derrida and Dufourmantelle, 2000: 149; see also Baker, 2009: 111). Therefore, sovereignty demands that primary obligations are met (like that of a state to protect its citizens) before secondary obligations can be (like that of welcoming strangers) (see Barnett, 2005: 13).

Precisely because sovereignty restrains, it enables hospitality to operate. Remember again Thaetetus and Xenos—hospitality could not be extended to Xenos without the sovereignty of Thaetetus and the state. The two enabling elements of sovereignty are:

1. "[T]he inescapable need for a decision" to be made "and responsibility for it to be taken." This need for a decision is how hospitality translates to practical politics—how "welcome might take concrete form" (Baker, 2009: 96, 118).
2. The fact that sovereignty by definition means having a home from which to offer hospitality. Hospitality necessitates opening a physical location that must be protected even as it is made vulnerable (Baker, 2009: 96, 118).[18]

Hence, hospitality in light of sovereignty demands a decision maker and a place to operate from: the state. Sovereignty grants a basis from which to practice hospitality, and sovereignty as enabled by the Westphalian system provides for the necessary security. Derrida, joined by Baker, identifies issues such as refugee resettlement and immigration as pertinent to hospitality and a now-made-vulnerable sovereign state. Hospitality needs to be practiced beyond borders as well. It is the power given to states by the Westphalian system that marks them as the insiders—thus, as insiders, they have the legitimacy (power) to be the sites of decision making in the international system. Since hospitality recognizes the state as a site of sovereignty and (now) insider-power, it accepts the state as a site of hospitality and also accepts it as an agent of hospitality. Drawing upon the examples of both ancient Greece (see Reus-Smit, 1999: 49) and early Christianity, hospitality can be practiced across borders and any actor with the ability to reasonably address requested needs should therefore do so.[19]

While Westphalia sets up in-groups and out-groups, the idea that this is always a negative may be a construction formed by IR scholars (see Brown, 2002: 21). States can still retain value even while other actors are granted more recognition, legitimacy, and the ability to act more circumspectly in international affairs, specifically toward failed states (see Barnett, 2005: 16). Abstraction does not have to occur just because a state is the primary actor, nor does a state *have to* engage in power (-over) politics. Westphalia can continue while political realism's emphasis on hard security and sovereignty is de-emphasized (not necessarily devalued). The state does not need to be made obsolete in order to practice proactive last resort; instead some of the Westphalian assumptions about sovereignty that coincide with legitimate authority and last resort need to be rethought. For instance, the global community can still agree that states have the primary responsibility to protect citizens through an emphasis upon human security.

Practicing Hospitality: Proactive Last Resort

Failed state conflicts pose a dilemma. Most people argue that something must be done, but states are constrained by the Westphalian norm of nonintervention (Johnson, 1999). In the past fifteen to twenty years, the concept of humanitarian intervention has been hotly contested and carried out with varying degrees of tempered enthusiasm and success. People are not only wary of Elshtain's humanitarian intervention, which is facilitated (ignobled) by American exceptionalism, but also of the emerging trend toward intervention in failed states becoming a new form of imperialism. A reconceptualization of last resort, based on hospitality, rests within a respect for those literal and figurative boundaries, which could allay such fears.

Historically, last resort was associated with political manipulations of and diplomatic forewarnings to the transgressor intended to enable the state, as the legitimate authority, to go to war justly. But what if last resort were injected with a healthy dose of pacifist proactivity? Bell argues that if the Just War tradition is a practice of Christian discipleship, last resort should be just that: "Last resort entails not simply asking when one may go to war but what one should do before war is even on the horizon to make the resort to war less likely" (2009: 192). Since the end of World War II, especially since the end of the Cold War, the motives and means of war have changed, and the Just War tradition needs to change with them. Without change, the tradition will be limited to addressing wars between state actors and will fail to address the majority of conflicts around the world in failed or weak states, which often involve humanitarian crises. The indicators introduced in chapter 2 inform international actors of where failed state conflicts are likely to occur. Use of these indicators as a means of proactivity can operate as a new modality for last resort.

If one thinks of *jus ad bellum*, *jus in bello*, and *jus post bellum* as happening along a timeline, last resort occurs perilously close to the actuality of war. But if *proactive* last resort based in hospitality were practiced, the timeline of Just (no) War avoids that peril. This is meant to suggest that forward-thinking last resort would eliminate the threat or possibility of war. This is not completely disconnected from Just War thinking. Just War *hopes* for peace as an outcome, and *jus ad bellum hopes* that war can be avoided. Fotion argues that Just War is used retrospectively and prospectively. A retrospective approach is used most often by "[h]istorians, political scientists, political commentators, ethicists, journalists, etc." to discuss what *has* happened, a hindsight-is-20/20 approach (Fotion, 2007: 30). But if one takes the lesser-used approach, the prospective approach, "[i]t might be supposed that the ideal time to employ [Just War] is before the start of the war. . . . [And] we [might] think that [Just War] should prevent war if it is to be good for anything" (Fotion, 2007: 30). There is very little difference, perhaps, between proactive and prospective Just War.

In Fotion's thorough examination of last resort, he makes additional contributions to this argument. First, he argues that last reasonable resort "can slow down the process of going to war" (Fotion, 2007: 114). Second, in *War and Ethics* (2007) he looks at applying an updated version of Just War to insurgent groups. In this setting, he argues that if the legitimate authority knows the insurgent group's grievances and demands, then addressing these in a reasonable manner before violence occurs is a form of last resort (Fotion, 2007: 105–6). There is very little difference between this and the concept of addressing the three types of weaknesses (see chapter 2) that indicate preconflict failed states or the need for military intervention for humanitarian purposes. There are many different methods, suggestions, policies, practices, and theories regarding how best to address these types of weaknesses—enough to fill several more volumes at least. Ideas proposed in chapter 2 include public diplomacy, international cooperation, holding multinational corporations accountable, and loosening restrictions on monies to be used for sustainable development. Plan Colombia will be returned to in the concluding chapter.

Still, each state and situation offers different challenges and each solution must depend upon the unique circumstances of that state. It is absurd to imagine that a better solution for Haiti would in any way be the same solution for Zimbabwe. Further, it must be emphasized that this will take *time*. One of the larger problems with the numerous post-1990 U.N. missions in Haiti has been their limited timeframes (Ward, 2006). In peace studies, John Paul Lederach (2010) believes conflict transformation will take decades, if not generations. Hospitality is the implementation of prescriptions that are truly transformative, proactive, and seeking the best for that particular state or community. Offering hospitality in a context where future conflict is indicated in a way that is not totalizing, colonizing, or imperialistic is proactive last resort.

It cannot be emphasized enough that hospitality—which moves political realism beyond military security, pushes pacifism toward transformative proactivity, and shifts the Just War tradition's focus from acute conflicts—rests on addressing the needs of others, as those in need identify them. Hospitality cannot be the imposition of *perceived* needs as determined by an interested actor, whether it is a multilateral response from the international community or regional actors, a single state actor, or a consortium of NGOs. Those that are in need must recognize this need and then ask for assistance in meeting the need. Otherwise, we verge on manipulation and power-over situations that are problematic to all involved.

Disinterested Hospitality

Although the legitimate authority criterion emerged before the Westphalian system did, it surely informed and was strengthened by the primacy of the state and its claim to sovereignty in this system. Although traditional and reinvigorated understandings of the Just War tradition may be of use in the state-to-state conflicts that happen with decreasing frequency each year, mainly by Global North countries against Global South countries (such as United States and Afghanistan and Iraq, or Russia and Georgia), these do not help one approach failed states. While weak or failed states are contestingly perceived as threatening the security of the Global North, they are a far more significant threat to those that live in them (Logan and Preble, 2006). To varying degrees of attention and success, these conflicts—such as in Haiti, Somalia, Yugoslavia, Rwanda, and Sierra Leone—are intervened upon by primarily Global North actors at the cost of complicated and expensive wars (humanitarian interventions). Yet humanitarian interventions—because of cost, perceived lack of self-interest, and the transgression of the Westphalian norm of nonintervention—are controversial foreign policy initiatives that strike disconcertingly close to neoimperialism. Instead, as an alternative, the reformulation of last resort addresses the known factors that indicate state crisis and failure, and thus can put off both failure and the possibility of humanitarian intervention.

If states accept the concept of human security and wish to practice hospitality, then these states must evaluate how they use power. Instead of a self-interested power-over, states must recognize the need for inverted self-interest, a form of disinterest. It is not out of self-interest that these actors operate but out of a responsibility *without* self-interest: for the neighbor. State actors must ignore whether or not this neighbor is perceived to be an enemy. If proactive last resort is only practiced toward friends or in order to make friends (as allies, giving aid for intelligence or security, or for what the new friend will do for the acting state), this will only create a manipulative power-over that is easier to do harm with or reject, or that may prevent actual good from happening.

Disinterested, no-strings-attached policies for the good of the other is the practice of hospitality rooted in the sovereignty of the decision-making state that acts within but also beyond borders. Hospitality reimagines sovereignty as a base from which to operate, and by operating within the Westphalian system, the ability to legitimately act in global affairs. Both proactive last resort and hospitality push against the absolutist confines of sovereignty because both seek regional or global security through intervention. As much as possible, proactive last resort policies need to address what is truly best for the people, the society, and the state *overall*. And, yes, this may be an impossible, naïve, fully unattainable idea—but does that mean no effort should go into such a goal?

CHAPTER SEVEN

———

A Liturgy

The same semester that I first studied nationalism and ethnic conflict as an undergraduate, with the Dayton Accords just behind us and peace in Northern Ireland a not-too-distant possibility, an assignment in my ethics class included Adrienne Rich's *What Is Found There* (1993). In it, Rich reprinted "To Peace," a poem by Suzanne Gardinier. It was a strikingly different articulation of the material I was reading in my other course. It begins,

> Peace I have feared you hated you scuffed dirt
> on what little of you I could bear near me

It continues,

>   . . . You have
> disgusted me slipping flowers into guns
> holding hands with yourself singing to bullets
> and dogs Who can speak your language but
> animals and saints What history records
> your triumphs . . .

It captures human frailty and anxiety, echoing the sentiments of IR's paradigm:

> In the land where you are loved what becomes
> of the veterans of all against all How
> will I clothe myself How will I eat How
> will I teach my children whom to respect
> how to find themselves on a map of the world
>
> . . .
>
> Tell me Bloodless Outlaw Phantom what is
> the work of the belligerent in
> your anarchic kingdom Where is my place
> (Gardinier, 1993: 61–62)

Those lines have stayed with me and have echoed through my mind as I wrote this book.

What has disturbed me in writing this book is that it would appear that Niebuhr, Hauerwas, and Elshtain all seem to fear peace, and fear erodes hospitality. Peace is too loose of a concept; too thick to achieve; too scary to achieve and therefore make oneself or one's country vulnerable—all fearful reasonings. Hauerwas' peace, apart from being defined by the Cross, is like an amoeba—constantly shifting and hard to pin down. At conferences, I have been told that peace is not the aim of Just War: war is. Yet if last resort measures work, they work by bringing peace—*jus ad bellum* is filled with fail-safe measures to avoid war in hopes of peace. In *jus in bello*, a better peace is the goal *after* the war. These both, then, make peace the goal. As Christians we say we know what peace is; ultimately we do. But we have a much harder time recognizing that as fragmented, imperfect, unknowing *creatures*, we humans will only ever be imperfect—in our speech, plans, and policy making—even when we are working toward peace. Yet because we know of and hope for a better peace, we cannot be afraid of trying to establish it *in this world*.

Calling attention to hegemonic Christianity in the United States and to complicity with it requires calling attention to how American

Christians fail to think critically about and act on structural force and power. As a security studies expert, hegemony is most apparent to me when I am looking at the subject of war, even though hegemony is everywhere. And American Christians are not necessarily afraid of their power and are sometimes naïvely unaware that they possess it. That Christians in the United States still see themselves as a persecuted population is a fascinating study in ignorance. Such positioning allows this population to comfortably retreat within its own communities. This means not only that they fail to engage a Christian's relationship with state power in the domestic and international arenas, but also that American Christians do not have conversations with those they might disagree with.

Such conversations can only take place surrounded by a spirit of hospitality. One way to disable complicity and reduce the power of hegemony is to truly engage in conversation and to hear and respect the other side's opinion. Hauerwas' engagement with his critics is one such example; the conversation he has with his friend and critic Romand Coles in their book, *Christianity, Democracy, and the Radical Ordinary* (2008), witnesses to a beautiful engagement in hospitality and vulnerability. Yet it is not just conversations between other Christians or fellow colleagues. Hospitality should also include having conversations with the people we disagree with the most—between theologians, security experts, policy makers, postmodern theorists, and feminist scholars. It is not necessarily easy to continue to hold our own truths at the center while listening and respecting others. But it is a way of being in relationship—as we are called to be. It does make us vulnerable—we may indeed end up letting go of some element of our belief system (without compromising on the truth at the center).

Unraveling Hegemonic Christianities

In all three strands of the Christians-and-war debate—realism versus pacifism versus Just War—there appears to be a serious resistance to seeing beyond one's particular perspective. This book brings out the commonalities between these three perspectives in order to seek answers in a contemporary setting. Each side recognizes the awesomeness of God's transcendence and his desire to be in relationship with his creation. They all comprehend the sacrifice of Christ on the Cross and the Trinity's performance of vulnerability. And they all desire to rectify injustices. Yet, these commonalities are sometimes lost when nuance is forgotten and narrow lenses are employed. Christian realists must be reminded of their call for social justice and that social justice reduces vulnerability on the margins. Pacifists need to be reminded of their call to find empathy for the other and that, even though Christians have all the time in the world to be followers of Christ, we do not have all the time in the world to help the hurting. Just War traditionalists need to be reminded that peace is the ultimate goal and that justice comes only from good practice: discipleship.

Christian hegemonic thinking operates in theological approaches to war by failing to hold itself accountable for complicity and failing to be critical of power in its many forms. Such failures marginalize regions and peoples in the world. Niebuhrian Christian realism does not fully acknowledge and appreciate the way Cold War politics and policies impacted the developing world as an unacknowledged population. Hauerwas' failure to be a proactive pacifist and to recognize his own privilege denies the obligation to act on behalf of the nonprivileged. Elshtain's justification of the Afghan war rests on disturbing assumptions about what it means to be a Muslim, and it is a betrayal of her call to speak against injustice. Encouraging these Christian traditions to offer hospitality unravels the hegemony, and it brings in the oppressed, subordinated, feared marginalized. Weakening the last resort criterion of the Just War tradition enables a proactive offer of hospitality to failing or failed states.

The Importance of Hospitality

Agape and hospitality reaffirm and bless the humanity of vulnerable populations. They acknowledge that, just as the self is vulnerable and thus anxious to find security, others are just as vulnerable and in need of security and care. Offering a place of welcome, hospitality brings others into relationship with the self. In international relations, this has often been conceived of as offering a site of welcome for refugees, asylum seekers, or immigrants. But hospitality needs to operate counterintuitively as well: states should take advantage of their power to help provide for human security in vulnerable places outside of their territory.

There must be a way to address some of the worst hurts in the world. Focusing on human security is a beginning. The poverty, malnourishment, lack of rights, poor governance, corruption, and militarization in failed states and the anarchic violence that brings genocide, rape, and other human rights violations have to be addressed. And they have to be addressed in ways that do not engender resentment, feed the fear of manipulation by outside forces, or subsume the conflict only to see it re-emerge in ten or thirty years. Hospitality's grounding in what is best for the other (what is best for the people in the failed states) instead of what is best for the self (those actors equipped and able to help) can alleviate some of these fears.

Last resort, the criterion that has never fully and effectively operated because it is defined so abstractly, provides a way for hospitality to operate beyond borders. I have written that I am "weakening" last resort. To Just War traditionalists that hold tightly to classic applications and definitions, this is true. But considering that last resort is so ineffective and therefore easily dismissed, I argue that this argument is strengthening last resort. Proactive last resort addresses the indicators of failing states. Since we know that failed states are either on the verge of or in conflict this knowledge makes addressing such indicators an imperative. It strengthens last resort by extending the last resort timeline to operate far in advance of a potential war or conflict, thereby reinforcing the ultimate Just War goal of a better peace.

This takes time. It means proactively examining indicators, maybe years in advance of an acute outbreak of violence. It may not be easy to sell to international actors, and it may reek of imperialistic intervention. Hospitality would require that international actors acknowledge a responsibility to others. And hospitality's care for the needs of others should soften the edge of intervention. Ultimately, proactive last resort is about helping the failed state find a way to become strong, competent, and protective of its inhabitants, which promotes the state's sovereignty. This cannot happen without a focus upon human security; a formerly failed state's sovereignty means nothing if provisions are not made to make its population better off. All of these measures lead away from negative to positive peace.

Finding one last maneuver before going to war could be dragged on indefinitely, so it is important to keep in mind that peace is the ultimate goal. If the proactive last resort measures do not work, then war is conceivably necessary to ensure the better peace that is the ultimate goal of the Just War tradition. War will happen in some cases. Nevertheless it is important to try for peace.

Future work on hospitality in IR does not have to remain focused upon failed states. There are a multitude of ways that hospitality can be applied and practiced. For instance, terrorism presents interesting and multidimensional problems. For example, when individuals have been extended the hospitality of the state and then attack it and its civilians, they have abused the state's trust. What is an ethical response on the part of the state? Another example is state terrorism. The manner in which Sri Lanka dealt with the political violence of the Liberation Tigers of Tamil Elam should be used as a lesson on what not to do. In this civil war, both sides were guilty of violence and destruction; but the Sri Lankan state arguably had a greater responsibility to bear in acting ethically. Although the terrorism (genocide and ethnic cleansing) employed by the state ended the conflict, it is expected that Tamilese political violence will re-emerge in the next generation. Additionally, as a transnational problem, solutions rooted in human security will demand cooperation on the part of international actors. Such cooperation is, in effect, hospitality. Thus, if cooperation is related to hospitality, then most transnational problems—not just political violence but environmental security and immigration, human rights, and shared resources issues—will have some relationship with hospitality.

A Return to Colombia

As much as Plan Colombia might look like proactive last resort, it is a distortion of what this book is hoping to achieve. It is not that all of Plan Colombia is bad—indeed, it is not: It was primarily Colombians who identified the needs and requested them in order to stave off a complete civil war. It engaged notions of human security and was rooted in the concept that Colombia could not enter a sustainable peace without addressing extreme poverty, environmental security, and human rights. It has worked—murder and kidnappings are down; FARC's and the ELN's activities have been curtailed; the connection between the military and the AUC and other right-wing paramilitaries are being revealed. The entity with the most power in this situation, however—the United States—has not acted hospitably.

In some senses, that last sentence is like a statement from a schoolmarm who is chastising the belligerent town drunk. It is a naïve, moralistic, and idealistic statement. Yet it is true. The United States failed to identify its own role in perpetuating the erosion of sovereignty in Colombia. It has failed to hold its own citizens accountable for the narcotics demand that funds and strengthens narcoterrorist organizations in Colombia. Instead, U.S. policies indicate that the government believes that narcoterrorism is a problem that can be dealt with by only addressing the supply side: production, distribution, and sales. This is unbalanced at best. At worst, addressing supply-side concerns puts the lives of impoverished Colombians at further risk. The heavy-handed military force used to attack the narcoterrorist groups and the coca barons puts civilians in the line of fire. Supporting aerial dusting of herbicide that is known to be toxic to people means accepting the deaths and illnesses of poor farmers and indigenous populations as collateral damage. These policies continue to see Colombia in the abstract: a large regional trading partner with a key asset: oil. To ignore Colombia's instability would have put the U.S. economy at further risk, especially after 2001's economic contraction.

To help make my point, I return to *The Girl in the Café*, the HBO movie mentioned at the start of chapter 1. Gina, the girl in the café, was invited by Lawrence, the repressed bureaucrat, to attend a fictional meeting of the G-8 in Reykjavik, Iceland. Gina is seemingly unable to keep herself from audaciously challenging the chancellor of the exchequer, and both the German and U.K. prime ministers about their commitment to the United Nations' Millennium Development Goals, intended to end extreme poverty. After Gina is forced to leave Reykjavik, Lawrence, knowing that he has lost all credibility, champions "the woman in question" by challenging his colleagues:

> I think we get in the habit of always compromising and therefore, we are always compromised. . . . If we were the men [sic] we all dreamed we'd be when we were young we'd be doing deals on all the other things [security, trade, and oil prices] and going home to explain our little failures to our countrymen, but we wouldn't compromise the actual lives of people we will never meet just because we'd never have to explain to them face-to-face why we didn't think it was worth fighting to stop them dying.

In the end, this inspires the United Kingdom's chancellor and prime minister to throw down the metaphorical gauntlet of shame to the other G-8 countries to give full support to the Millennium Development Goals, which is, of course, what happens. Yes, this is a wonderful Hollywood ending tempered only by the sound of fingers snapping every three seconds as the credits roll to symbolize the death of a child from malnourishment. Using proactive last resort as an umbrella for a multitude of policies toward failed states allows various actors in the international system to not compromise or accept failure when it comes to addressing those in the margins in global affairs.

Plan Colombia was a compromise, and therefore it compromised Colombians. It also compromised the United States. Instead of acting selflessly and disinterestedly in what was best for Colombia, the United States acted within political realism's paradigm: self-interestedly. A scholar of IR could just accept this. Or a scholar of IR deeply committed to the best interests of people could contest it. What might a hospitable Plan Colombia have looked like? First, the United States, as the primary aid giver, would have held itself responsible for contributing to Colombia's insecurity. This might have included creating domestic programs to deter narcotics usage. The government would properly monitor the terms of the Leahy Amendment and stop turning a blind eye to human rights abuses. This might be served by working closely with NGOs, such as Amnesty International, Human Rights Watch, and the International Committee of the Red Cross. This would contribute to regaining the trust of the international community in Plan Colombia. The United States would better monitor the aid money and find a way of guaranteeing that it would not go to paramilitaries.

Second, it would have respected the original request for an aid package that had a greater emphasis on human security. Military aid would still have comprised a majority of the package, but not 80 percent. The 35 percent difference in funding could have gone to a more rapid transformation of the judicial system and to strengthening the rule of law. Instead of opting to spray illicit crops, the United States could have opted to address why indigenous and itinerate farmers were choosing to grow them, creating a sustainable and literally healthier solution. Recognizing that licit crops do not yield as significant of a profit as illicit crops, funding programs to help subsidize farmer's incomes might have been more helpful, especially since the United States and the West heavily subsidize their own farming industries, making it more difficult for those in the Global South to be sustainably competitive. More money could have gone to urban employment via foreign direct investment, and educational programs could have helped keep people out of the drug trade. In the aid and training granted to the military and police forces, there should have more focus on the Geneva Conventions and respect for human rights.

All of this might have taken more time and not yielded results as quickly, but immediate results may be too high of an expectation. For instance, after the Cold War, scholars and policy makers expected that Eastern Europe would be transformed overnight, or at least very quickly; but for countries shaking off forty or fifty years of Soviet communism, the transformation would not, could not, happen overnight. The same is true of Colombia—true, lasting change will take some time. Further, without respecting human rights and addressing the root causes of narcotics production, grievances against those with power and privilege will grow. This echoes Sri Lanka: a state cannot brutally rid itself of a problem without anticipating that the problem will return at some point. Addressing the ills that cause human insecurity and making true lasting change allow for a sustainable peace to emerge.

A Liturgy

According to Emmanuel Levinas, when the powerful sacrificially relate to others, they are engaging and/or performing a liturgy. In a Christian service, the liturgy is a pattern for worship. For Christians, allowing Levinas to break them out of their mold means ceasing to hold the liturgy just to the duration of the service—that is, time in the church as a time of worship—and seeing that activity in the world, outside of church, is equally liturgical. For the most part, Christians do this well. Yet American Christians arguably have a difficult time relating their work to international politics and knowing how best to respond to war, especially in humble ways. It is not easy to break with tradition; it is not easy to move outside of what is known. Yet nothing gets better if nothing changes. Hospitality has never been about doing what is easy: welcoming strangers into the home without knowing their origins or intentions is distinctly uncomfortable. It is easy to envision the hosts sweating anxiously until more information was given, because their sovereign safe place has been transgressed.

In IR, sovereignty is the prize. But what kind of prize is it when everything inside is being destroyed? We do not watch a house burn and do nothing. Even though a house is the inhabitant's sovereign space, the surrounding community values what might be inside: human life. Of lesser importance are the contents, which may still be of great importance to the owners. If the house is in a neighborhood, it may not be the only house to burn. Why should sovereignty enable the international community to stand aside as a state burns? We value the life inside; we value the contents (think of the ancient Buddhas in Afghanistan); we value regional and international stability. There are measures in place now for dealing with failed states, from NGO responses, to past NATO interventions, to R2P. Yet none of them work well or extensively enough to present the international community with a hospitable, proactive response that truly helps avoid war. No matter how different each response may be, it is a liturgical response to crisis, marginality, and vulnerability.

Notes

Introduction

1. All quotations from the Bible are from the New International Version.

2. While not making this exact argument, the U.S. Catholic Bishops in their "Pastoral Letter on War and Peace," on nuclear disarmament, come close to this (1983).

Chapter 1. Harming Others

1. This is a very long and complex argument that I have foreshortened in the interest of space. For more in-depth articulations of this argument, see, among others, Tickner, 2001, 1992; Enloe, 2000, 1989, 1983; Sylvester, 2002, 1990.

2. Niebuhr graced the cover of *Time* at the beginning of the Cold War, on the 8 March 1948 issue. At a time of great anxiety, Hauerwas was named "America's Best Theologian" by *Time* in its 17 September 2001 issue. Elshtain was one of the main signatories to the letter "What We Are Fighting For," published in American newspapers in 2002 (see Elshtain, 2004: 193–218).

3. In striking contrast is James Turner Johnson's approach to Christian realism in his scholarly work on the Just War tradition. He frequently engages

Christian realism and Reinhold Niebuhr, seeing them as sympathetic to the tradition and not at odds with it (see Johnson 2011, 1999, and 1981).

4. Ironically, this aligns with Niebuhr's own thinking.

5. Additionally, Jesus does not directly confront the Romans because they are not responsible for daily life; instead it is more appropriate to address the Jewish leaders (Stassen, 2006: 153).

6. Even Jesus, being subject to the Roman Empire, was complicit "in the horrors wrought by Rome" (Adams, 2006: 71).

Chapter 2. **Marginal Wars**

1. Old wars are related to the development of the Westphalian system and to the evolution of the Just War tradition. They were fought in Europe between the fifteenth and eighteenth centuries (Kaldor, 1999: 13). These wars were part of "the same phenomenon: a construction of the centralized, 'rationalized,' hierarchically ordered, territorialized modern state" (Kaldor, 1999: 15). During this extended time period, states were the legitimate authorities with established standing armies paid for via taxes raised by the bureaucracy. From this the state's monopoly on violence developed, which was "intrinsic" to the supplanting of *jus ad bellum* and the reliance upon *raison d'état* (Kaldor, 1999: 16–17).

2. Militarization happens where countries have high defense spending as a ratio of their gross national income and disproportionately large armies in relation to their population. It may also include the cultural impact of military spending.

3. This leads to possible frustration and subsequent recruitment by militant organizations.

4. Resistance may happen because the state fears that interference may exacerbate the problem or that outside interference lends credibility and legitimacy to secessionist or anti-government forces (ICISS, 2001: 25).

5. Both of these organizations, however, are often criticized for upholding the self-interest of the United States and the developed West.

6. The Canadian response to human security was the creation of the Responsibility to Protect (R2P), which uses Just War theorizing to justify an intervention for humanitarian purposes (ICISS, 2001). It is promising because R2P has addressed the issue of sovereignty in a way that aligns nicely with hospitality. Instead of the United Nations acting in every instance, R2P provides

guidelines that recognize a state's sovereignty, which is negated only when the state can no longer maintain or abandons its responsibility to protect people within its borders (ICISS, 2001: 7–8). Further, R2P's commitment to preventative multilateral action is very important (ICISS, 2001: 22–25). Nonetheless, it is arguably too late. R2P rests on ideas of responsibility for humans' well-being, but it does so in a war setting.

7. This is true even if there are those who would propose a new era of imperialism as a good (see Mallaby, 2002; Cooper, 2002).

8. Dirty wars, or *guerra sucia*, are wars conducted by clandestine agents of the state. They typically refer to the internal conflicts that took place in Latin America during the postcolonial period.

9. This may be changing. Recently, the Obama Administration said that it would limit the amount of military aid and increase the amount of humanitarian aid.

10. Glen Stassen's Just Peacemaking theory encompasses similar ideas: confrontation of power, sustainable development, and respect for human rights. Yet his ideas stay rooted within pacifism and nonviolence, whereas I believe that there are times that war may be a necessary action. Furthermore, Stassen tends to engage a liberal peace argument, conflating peace with democracy (Stassen, 2006).

11. Development can happen in a variety of ways—there are plenty of differing opinions, from Jeffrey Sachs (2005) and Paul Collier (2003) to Dambisa Moyo (2009)—but any development solution must be tailored to each state.

Chapter 3. **Hospitality toward Others**

1. Since the Enlightenment, Western political thought has been dependent upon idealizations of the political actor (traditionally constructed as Western, white, rational men) as fully autonomous—able to make (rational) decisions with no constraint placed upon it (him) (see Toulmin, 1990). It is clearly gendered to favor men as political actors with rational agency. The idea of a completely autonomous individual is false. Owing to social, political, and cultural structures, an individual's choices and agency are limited and/or dependent upon access to certain choices, or lack thereof. Thus, it is more accurate to discuss agency in decision making to relational autonomy (Hirschmann, 1992; Sylvester, 2002).

2. The states that do not have security are already so reliant upon outside help from NGOs, IGOs, and other governments that they have already foregone the sovereignty that security is meant to protect (see Balaam and Veseth, 2008: 175–90).

3. Collective security is the recognition, typically through formal agreements and treaties, of mutual security or the knowledge that each state can and may be affected by the security threats faced by another. It is codified in several places, including Charter 5 of the North Atlantic Treaty, which NATO invoked for the first time after the 9/11 attacks on the United States. It is strongly related to liberal idealism, another mainstream theory in IR, which believes in cooperation, collaboration, and the idea that peace can be found by strengthening international institutions (as opposed to political realism).

4. These threats may be direct, such as state-sponsored terrorism, but may also be indirect, such as refugees from a failed state (Farah, 2006).

Chapter 4. **The Invulnerability Myth**

1. In a personal conversation between Nick Rengger and Kenneth Waltz at a conference in Waltz's honor ("The King of Thought," University of Aberystwyth, Aberystwyth, Wales, September 2008), he told Nick Rengger that it was never his intention to create a new strain of political realism. Instead, his aim was to have a conversation to correct some missteps within political realism as he saw them (Rengger, 2012).

2. Marilyn McCord Adams' *Christ and Horrors* (2006) holds a different perspective on this subject. Humans are fragmented and limited creatures, but such a condition is not a result of the Fall but rather a condition of precompletion. She argues that God made the world incomplete, meaning that there is a mismatch between material creation and human needs, bringing about "horrors," the radical mismatches that exist in human life, for example, between human hunger and the limited access to the world's food supply. Such horrors lead us into a more intimate relationship with God. Adams argues that God does not view horrors unsympathetically. As a testament to His sympathy, God sent the Word to both participate in and become victim of the horrors, which brings reconciliation between ourselves and God (Adams, 2006).

3. The international system is anarchic because there is no form of global governance that can make resolutions binding. Thus, states exist in a "state

of nature" similar to the Hobbesian pre–social contract state of nature (see Brown, 1997: 106–26; Waltz, 1959: 159–86).

4. Some people believe that unipolarity is a safer balance of power, such as those who advocate hegemonic stability theory (Webb and Krasner, 1989), and some believe that bipolarity is safer, for instance those who might refer to the Cold War as the "Long Peace" (Gaddis, 1987).

5. To Niebuhr, the development of nuclear weaponry was yet another failure of the liberal agenda that demonstrated that humans cannot triumph over "natural forces" but that progress "increases the possibilities of both good and evil"—which is perfectly evident in the development of nuclear power (Niebuhr, 1961: 23).

6. Niebuhr defines pragmatism as "the application of Christian freedom and a sense of responsibility to the complex issues of economics and politics, with a firm resolve that inherited dogmas and generalizations will not be accepted no matter how revered or venerable, if they do not contribute to the establishment of justice in a given situation" (Niebuhr, 1957: 253).

7. For more information on these criticisms see Moser and Clark, 2001; Enloe, 2000; 1989; Sylvester, 1999.

8. Jürgen Moltmann also examines the dualism in *kenosis* and seeks to overcome this valuing of one over the other. Moltmann argues that in Christ's death on the Cross "he is completely with himself and completely with the other, the man who is dehumanized" (1974: 205). Further, Moltmann finds that Christianity has tried to exclude aspects of the divine from the suffering on the Cross. This is deeply problematic because it keeps God and the Trinity outside of suffering and death. But precisely because Christ as a member of the Trinity suffered, God suffers with humans as an act of love and thus "[d]ying no longer alienates man and God" (emphasis removed) (Moltmann, 1974: 214–15, 217). In reference to this argument on the dehumanized, subjugated other: "God became man that dehumanized [persons] might become true [persons]. We become true [persons] in the community of the incarnate, the suffering and loving, the human God. This salvation, too, is outwardly permanent, and immortal in the humanity of God, but in itself it is a new life full of inner movement, with suffering and joy, love, and pain, taking and giving; it is changeableness in the sense of life to its highest possible degree" (Moltmann, 1974: 231).

9. Volf also addresses this by bringing in Ulrich Beck's concept of a "risk society," where risk is now manufactured by humans as opposed to nature.

These risks can range from environmental degradation to nuclear weaponry—in other words, it is a larger conceptualization of the security dilemma (see Volf, 2008; Beck, 1992).

10. Lovin's updating of Christian realism, however, leaves something to be desired. Lovin acknowledges that state sovereignty is challenged and that power is no longer just state-to-state, thus he argues Christian realism should now take into account the transformative nature of globalization (Lovin, 2007). But this is just another form of abstraction that keeps power concentrated at the state or suprastate level without recognizing how power on the international level affects the lives of people.

11. This is true even if "post-9/11" is a discursive maneuver used to justify and find support for problematic counterterrorism policies (see Jackson, 2005).

12. The fears of loose nukes and fissile material getting into the wrong hands, though, may be overblown (Walker, 2000).

13. It is too simplistic to suggest that the trillions of dollars spent on nuclear weapons would have instead been spent on aid to developing countries if the nuclear arms race had never occurred. But it is still money that may have been spent on ways that encouraged development and economic growth worldwide.

Chapter 5. **The Presence of Suffering**

1. Oliver Richmond argues that definitions of peace are often "totalizing" and that if one subscribes only to "liberal peace," meaning a peace that is based upon liberal institutions of democracy and capitalism, then this can be seen as a power-over maneuver that (re)-colonizes areas in conflict. Instead, Richmond argues, there may be multiple roads to peace that are not so hegemonic (2008 and 2002).

2. Galtung was the first to articulate the problem of structural violence, and he published it early in the history of peace studies in *The Journal of Peace Research* in 1969.

3. The concept of *ahimsa* was "interpreted by [Gandhi] as meaning individual and social love in thought and deed, if possible, for all beings" (Power, 1963: 99; see also Elliott, 1980: 31).

4. Why is it that I decided not to focus on Yoder in this chapter? After all, Hauerwas is his protégé. As I argued in chapter 1, Hauerwas has claimed

a larger space in the American psyche, which places him alongside Niebuhr and Elshtain. Still, Yoder, as a Mennonite and a man of deep faith, argued that God used Jesus to work in people's lives, transforming society. Since God will use Christians as He wishes, Christians are meant to not take over or become agents of the world, but to stay rooted in their faith as a method for transformation (1978).

5. However, the conflict in Nigeria or the conflicts along the fault line between the heavily Muslim northern Africa and the predominantly Christian southern Africa (even though both religions are infused with African religions) are constructed. A recent Pew Forum on Religion and Public Life survey reveals that to label religion as the cause of the violence is a simplification. The people in these areas are more concerned with socio-economic factors and are more tolerant of other beliefs than originally thought (Pew Forum, 2010).

6. Glen Stassen makes a similar argument: it may be the job of governments to sometimes make war, but it is always the responsibility of Christians to follow the nonviolent teachings of Christ (Stassen, 2005: 288).

7. Hauerwas claims that such witness can be multicultural and nondomineering with this statement: "The invitation to join such a life [Christianity] is made not on the assumption that there is something wrong with the others' beliefs. . . . We are not sinners because we are Hindu, Muslim, secularist, or Christian, but because we are people who live as though we can be our own creator and redeemer" (Hauerwas, 1981: 105). As with Niebuhr, the ultimate problem in human nature is to deny our finitude.

8. Horrors themselves are often delineated as distinctly political events, for example, racism, sexism, nationalism, and genocide. Bringing up the raping and mutilation of women (Adams, 2006: 39) leads me to the horrors attendant in failed state conflicts of Rwanda, Sierra Leone, Sudan, Uganda, the former Yugoslavia, and Chechnya. Torture to disintegrate a personality echoes the current debate in the U.S. over treatment of prisoners of war, noncombatants, and enemy combatants (Adams, 2006: 39). Other political circumstances Adams lists are Nazi death camps and the ethics of nuclear weapons (Adams, 2006: 39).

9. If such a statement is accepted uncritically, Coles worries that this means that Christians then create an imaginary vision/version of the church in which it is perfect and the world is not. In such perfection, Coles wonders whether the Christians would see themselves only "as the footwashers," never needing their own feet to be washed in turn (Hauerwas and Coles, 2008: 212).

10. This could, for instance, be related to Hauerwas' accusation that Niebuhr has tried to make his theology relevant to the world (Hauerwas, 2001: 36–39).

11. For instance, even though Hauerwas clearly defines the church against the world in *Community of Character* (see above), he still argues that the church breaks down boundaries: "The most striking social ethical fact about the church is that the story of Jesus provides the basis to break down arbitrary and false boundaries between people" (Hauerwas, 1981: 51).

12. I would argue that even though Hauerwas is Cross-centered, his narrative theology focuses on the life and death of Jesus more than on the resurrection.

13. The politics of death results from the monopoly of violence the liberal state possesses that is aided by fear (Hauerwas and Coles, 2008: 7). For Hauerwas, the politics/culture of death is a direct outcome of liberalism, modernity, and Constantinianism. The culture of death, an outcome conceivably of the politics of death, encompasses the practices of "abortion, suicide, capital punishment, and war" (Hauerwas, 2001: 231). Such practices are a result of modernity, because modernity proposes a world in which "God does not matter" (Hauerwas, 2001: 231). Hauerwas' 2001 Gifford Lectures establish that as theologians—specifically William James and Niebuhr—began to engage in the suppositions of modernity and liberalism, they began to deny God's supremacy. Such engagements move the church away from its necessary focus upon the Cross and have tried to "make Christianity at home in the world" (Hauerwas, 2001: 33). Hauerwas concludes that Niebuhr, having lived a political life, attempted to create "an account of liberal Christianity acceptable to a liberal culture and politics" (Hauerwas, 2001: 88). Like I do, Hauerwas finds that Niebuhr has placed too much emphasis on the actuality of the world instead of hopeful possibilities.

14. It should be noted that this dovetails quite interestingly with Niebuhrian thought about human pride as well.

15. Some clarity would be helpful here because in the introductory chapter of *Christianity, Democracy, and the Radical Ordinary* there is some ambiguity about how much in the book as a whole Hauerwas actually agrees with. Almost as a disclaimer, Hauerwas says the book is more Coles, and even in it, Coles sometimes suggests that he's not sure what Hauerwas agrees with and to what extent (2008: 12–15).

16. For instance, the Failed State Index measures "Group Grievance" (based on injustices), "Delegitimation of the State" (criminalization of the state

or mistrust in it), as well as the suspension of the rule of law (Fund for Peace, 2010).

Chapter 6. The Offer of Hospitality

1. The idea that the Just War tradition provides an intermediate solution between realism and pacifism is not new (Elshtain, 2004: 50–57; U.S. Catholic Bishops, 1983).

2. Fotion articulates that Just War is an ambiguous theory that stands as a "family name for various theories about the ethics of war" (Fotion, 2007: 10).

3. For example, during the early 1990s, the sanctions against Haiti led to food and job scarcity and declines in nutrition, immunizations, clean water, and access to medical care. They were associated with a 20 percent rise in an already high rate of mortality in children under five. Malnourishment in children rose from 5 percent to 23 percent between 1991 and 1992 alone (Garfield, 2002).

4. Clausewitz believed war tended to extremes (Kaldor, 1999: 19–21). Or, as Michael Walzer eloquently stated about Clausewitzian thought, "there can be no imaginable act of violence, however treacherous and cruel, that falls outside of war, that is not-war, for the logic of war simply is a steady thrust toward moral extremity" (Walzer, 1977: 23).

5. On Clausewitz, see Kaldor, 1999: 15–25; Bellamy, 2005: 275; Johnson, 1999: 19.

6. Even H. Richard Niebuhr "rejected traditional Just War criteria, insisting that normal values were absolute and that all could be sacrificed in order to protect other values" (Bellamy, 2008: 106).

7. George Lopez and David Cortright, however, argue that embargoes were effective in the 1990s for keeping Iraq contained (2004).

8. For example, according to Bell, for the Just War tradition to truly be of use to the world, the *entirety* of the church should speak with one voice.

9. According to a Google Scholar search, Elshtain's *Just War against Terror* is cited 281 times. The first edition was published in 2003 and the second edition in 2004. The most cited work of James Turner Johnson is his 1981 book, *The Just War Tradition and the Restraint of War*, at 180 times. Paul Ramsey's 2002 book (originally published in 1968) on Just War is cited 233 times, while his classic *Basic Christian Ethics* (1954) is cited 239 times. Bell's 2009 book, *Just War as Christian Discipleship*, is cited once.

10. The Tupamaros were a Marxist-Leninist, urban-guerrilla, revolutionary organization that operated in the 1960s and 1970s in Uruguay, mainly in Montevideo.

11. This is actually a rather large debate in terrorism studies currently. For more on this debate see Held, 2011; Bellamy, 2005; Ganor, 2005; Jackson, 2005.

12. Elshtain created the designations "Just Warrior" and "Beautiful Soul" to deconstruct gendered manipulations of virtue and legitimacy-as-granted-via-citizenship.

13. Ramsey states that Augustine "[b]lunt[s] the edge of" *agape* because "the neighbor is loved *because* he is righteous" and not for his/her own sake (Ransey 1954: 120–21).

14. Sauron is the main antagonist in J. R. R. Tolkein's *The Lord of the Rings* trilogy. Sauron craves absolute power and domination, and his power is dependent upon the One Ring, which has been lost to him. Possession of the One Ring would enable Sauron to have control over all free people.

15. This is not without problems. The conflation of the *sovereign state* with moral authority leaves other actors without any moral authority and political legitimacy. This cannot always be true—IGOs, NGOs, and substate actors should have access to both. Further, if IR unquestionably grants this to states, we fail to regard when states transgress moral limits, as in state terrorism or illegitimate violence against other states, as in the Iraq War.

16. James Turner Johnson also makes this argument: "The conception of sovereignty as moral responsibility in the classic just war tradition contrasts importantly with the morally sterile concept of sovereignty in the Westphalian system" (2005).

17. Westphalian system norms include nonintervention, nonaggression, and the monopoly on violence.

18. Clive Barnett argues that to Derrida hospitality cannot be an "irrecusable obligation to generalized others" because then existing obligations may be negated or neglected. Thus, if a stranger poses a direct and obvious threat, s/he cannot be made welcome because the government's existing responsibility is to the security of its citizens (Barnett, 2005: 12–13).

19. The International Commission on Intervention and State Sovereignty articulation of the United Nations' "responsibility to protect" is a similar argument (ICISS, 2001).

Bibliography

Adams, Marilyn McCord. 2006. *Christ and Horrors: The Coherence of Christology*. Cambridge: Cambridge University Press.

Ahmed, Leila. 1992. *Women and Gender in Islam: Historical Roots of a Modern Debate*. New Haven: Yale University Press.

Akram, Susan Mussarat. 2000. "Orientalism Revisited in Asylum and Refugee Claims." *International Journal of Refugee Law* 12 (1): 7–40.

Amnesty International. 2011. "Annual Report 2011: Colombia." http://www .amnesty.org/en/region/colombia/report-2011.

Andolsen, Barbara Hilkert. 1994. "*Agape* in Feminist Ethics." In *Feminist Theological Ethics: A Reader*, ed. Lois K. Daly, 146–59. Louisville: Westminster/John Knox Press.

———. 1981. "*Agape* in Feminist Ethics." *Journal of Religious Ethics* 9 (1): 69–83.

Andreas, Peter. 2005. "Criminalizing Consequences of Sanctions: Embargo Busting and Its Legacy." *International Studies Quarterly* 49: 335–60.

Aquinas, Thomas. 2007. *Summa Theologica*. Intratext Digital Library. Print source, Benziger Bros. ed., 1947. http://www.intratext.com/x/eng0023 .htm.

Arterbury, Andrew. 2007. "Entertaining Angels: Hospitality in Luke and Acts." *Christian Reflection: A Series in Faith and Ethics* 25: 20–26. Waco: Center for Christian Ethics, Baylor University.

Augustine. 1996. *The Political Writings*. Introduction by Henry Paolucci. Washington, DC: Regnery Publishing.

Aung San Suu Kyi. 1995. "Freedom, Development, and Human Worth." *Journal of Democracy,* 6 (2): 11–19.

———. 1992. "In Quest of Democracy." *Journal of Democracy* 3 (1): 5–14.

Bacevich, Andrew. 2008a. "Present at the Re-Creation: A Neoconservative Moves On." *Foreign Affairs* (July/August). http://www.foreignaffairs.com/articles/64466/andrew-j-bacevich/present-at-the-re-creation.

———. 2008b. "Illusions of Managing History: The Enduring Relevance of Reinhold Niebuhr." *Bill Moyers Journal,* 15 August. http://www.pbs.org/moyers/journal/08152008/profile3.html.

———. 2005. *The New American Militarism*. Oxford: Oxford University Press.

Baker, Gideon. 2009. "The Politics of Hospitality: Sovereignty and Ethics in Political Community." In *The Future of Political Community*, ed. Gideon Baker and Jens Bartelson, 51–70. London: Routledge.

Balaam, David N., and Michael Veseth. 2008. *Introduction to International Political Economy*. 4th ed. Upper Saddle River, NJ: Pearson/Prentice Hall.

Barash, David P., and Charles P. Webel. 2008. *Peace and Conflict Studies*. Thousand Oaks, CA: Sage.

Barber, Benjamin. 1996. *Jihad vs. McWorld*. New York: Ballantine Books.

Barnett, Clive. 2005. "Ways of Relating: Hospitality and the Acknowledgement of Otherness." *Progress in Human Geography* 29 (1): 5–21.

Barnett, Michael N. 2002. *Eyewitness to a Genocide: The United Nations and Rwanda*. Ithaca: Cornell University Press.

Bates, Thomas R. 1975. "Gramsci and the Theory of Hegemony." *Journal of the History of Ideas* 36 (2): 351–66.

Beck, Ulrich. 1992. *Risk Society: Towards a New Modernity*. Thousand Oaks, CA: Sage.

Beckman, Peter, and Francine J. D'Amico. 1994. *Women, Gender, and World Politics*. Westport: Greenwood.

Bell, Daniel M., Jr. 2009. *Just War as Christian Discipleship: Recentering the Tradition in the Church Rather Than the State*. Grand Rapids: Brazos Press.

———. 2007. "The Politics of Fear and the Gospel of Love." *Journal for Cultural and Religious Theory* 8 (2): 55–80.

———. 2006. "Can a War Against Terror Be Just?" *Crosscurrents* 56 (1): 34–45.

Bellamy, Alex J. 2008. *Just Wars: From Cicero to Iraq*. London: Polity Press.

————. 2005. "Is the War on Terror Just?" *International Relations* 19 (3): 275–96.

Berdal, Mats, and David M. Malone. 2000. *Greed and Grievance: Economic Agendas in Civil Wars*. Boulder: Lynne Rienner.

Berger, Kevin. 2007. "The Iraqi Insurgency for Beginners." Salon.com, 2 March. http://www.salon.com/2007/03/02/insurgency_3/.

Bergoffen, Debra B. 2008. "The Just War Tradition: Translating the Ethics of Human Dignity into Political Practices." *Hypatia* 23 (2): 72–94.

Blanchard, Eric. 2003. "Gender, International Relations, and the Development of Feminist Security Theory." *Signs* 28 (4): 1289–312.

Bobcock, Robert. 1986. *Hegemony*. London: Tavistock.

Bova, Russell. 2010. *How the World Works*. Upper Saddle River, NJ: Pearson Education.

Brown, Chris. 2002. *Sovereignty, Rights, and Justice: International Political Theory Today*. London: Polity Press.

————. 1997. *Understanding International Relations*. New York: Palgrave.

Bull, Hedley. 1977. *The Anarchical Society*. New York: Columbia University Press.

Butler, Judith. 2009. *Frames of War: When Is Life Grievable?* London: Verso Books.

————. 2004. *Undoing Gender*. London: Routledge.

————. 1993. *Bodies That Matter: On the Discursive Limits of Sex*. London: Routledge.

————. 1990. *Gender Trouble: Feminism and the Subversion of Identity*. London: Routledge.

Cahill, Lisa Sowle. 1992. "Theological Contexts of Just War Theory and Pacifism: A Response to J. Bryan Hehir." *Journal of Religious Ethics* 20 (2): 259–65.

CAIR (Council on American Islamic Relations). 2007. "Response to September 11, 2001 Attacks." 28 March. http://www.cair.com/Portals/0/pdf/September_11_statements.pdf.

————. 2001. "CAIR's Anti-Terrorism Campaigns." 11 September. http://www.cair.com/AmericanMuslims/AntiTerrorism/ISNAJoinsAMPCCinCondemningTerroristAttacks.aspx.

Carrigan, T. R., W. Connell, and J. Lee. 1985. "Towards a New Sociology of Masculinity." *Theory and Society* 14 (5): 551–604.

Charles, J. Daryl. 2005. *Between Pacifism and Jihad: Just War and Christian Tradition*. Downer's Grove, IL: InterVarsity Press.

Chesterman, Simón. 2002. *Just War or Just Peace? Humanitarian Intervention and International Law.* Oxford: Oxford University Press.

Childress, James F. 1992. "Just War Criteria." In *War in the Twentieth Century: Sources in Theological Ethics,* ed. Richard B. Miller, 351–72. Louisville: Westminster/John Knox Press.

———. 1982. "Just War Criteria." In *Moral Responsibility in Conflicts: Essays on Non-Violence, War, and Conscience,* ed. James F. Childress. Baton Rouge: Louisiana State University Press.

Chua, Amy. 2003. *World on Fire.* New York: Anchor Books.

CNN. 2005. "U.S. Dismisses Call for Chavez's Killing." CNN.com, 24 August. http://www.cnn.com/2005/US/08/23/robertson.chavez/.

Coakley, Sarah. 2002. *Powers and Submissions: Spirituality, Philosophy, and Gender.* Malden: Blackwell.

Collier, Paul. 2003. *Breaking the Conflict Trap: Civil War and Development Policy.* Washington, DC: World Bank Publications.

Conflict Prevention and Reconstruction Team. 2005. "Conflict Analysis Framework." World Bank. http://siteresources.worldbank.org/INTCPR/214574-1112883508044/20657757/CAFApril2005.pdf.

Connell, R. W. 1995. *Masculinities.* Berkeley: University of California Press.

———. 1987. *Gender and Power: Society, the Person, and Sexual Politics.* Stanford: Stanford University Press.

Connell, R. W., and James W. Messerschmidt. 2005. "Hegemonic Masculinity: Rethinking the Concept." *Gender and Society* 19 (6): 829–59.

Cooper, Marc. 2001. "Plan Colombia." *The Nation,* 19 March. http://www.thenation.com/article/plan-colombia.

Cooper, Robert. 2002. "The New Liberal Imperialism." *The Observer,* 7 April. http://attacberlin.de/fileadmin/Sommerakademie/Cooper_New_liberal_Imperialism.pdf.

Cortright, David. 2010. "Thinking and Teaching About the Social Change Around Us." Lecture given at Teaching Peace in the 21st Century Summer Institute for Faculty, Kroc Institute, University of Notre Dame, 17 June.

———, ed. 1997. *The Price of Peace: Incentives and International Conflict Prevention.* New York: Rowman and Littlefield.

Cortright, David, and George Lopez. 2004. "Containing Iraq: Sanctions Worked." *Foreign Affairs* (July/August). http://s06.middlebury.edu/ECON0340A/Containing%20Iraq.pdf.

Crenshaw, Martha. 1995. "The Effectiveness of Terrorism in the Algerian War." In *Terrorism in Context*, ed. Martha Crenshaw, 473–513. University Park: Pennsylvania State University Press.

Curtis, Richard. 2005. *The Girl in the Café*. Screenplay. Directed by David Yates. HBO Video.

D'Amico, Francine. 2007. "Women National Leaders: Paths to Power." Paper given at the International Studies Association 48th Annual Convention, Chicago, 28 February.

Deane, Herbert A. 1963. *The Political and Social Ideas of Saint Augustine*. New York: Columbia University Press.

Deede Johnson, Kristen. 2007. *Theology, Political Theory, and Pluralism: Beyond Tolerance and Difference*. Cambridge: Cambridge University Press.

Denike, Margaret. 2008. "The Human Rights of Others: Sovereignty, Legitimacy, and 'Just Causes' for the 'War on Terror.'" *Hypatia* 23 (2): 95–121.

Derrida, Jacques. 2001. *On Cosmopolitanism and Forgiveness*. London: Routledge.

Derrida, Jacques, and Anne Dufourmantelle. 2000. *Of Hospitality: Anne Dufourmantelle Invites Jacques Derrida to Respond*. Trans. Rachel Bowlby. Stanford: Stanford University Press.

Eberle, Christopher J. 2006. "Religion, Pacifism, and the Doctrine of Restraint." *Journal of Religious Ethics* 34 (2): 203–24.

Eckert, Amy. 2009. "Outsourcing War." In *Rethinking the 21st Century: "New" Problems, "Old" Solutions*, ed. Amy Eckert and Laura Sjoberg, 136–54. London: Zed Books.

Eisenhower, Dwight D. 1953. "Atoms for Peace." Address given to the 470th Plenary Meeting of the United Nations General Assembly. Vienna: International Atomic Energy Agency, 8 December. http://www.iaea.org /About/history_speech.html.

Elliott, Gregory C. 1980. "Components of Pacifism: Conceptualization and Measurement." *Journal of Conflict Resolution* 24 (1): 27–54.

Elshtain, Jean Bethke. 2008. *Sovereignty: God, State, and Self*. New York: Basic Books.

———. 2004. *The Just War Against Terror: The Burden of American Power in a Violent World*. 2nd ed. New York: Basic Books.

———. 2000. *Who Are We? Critical Reflections and Hopeful Possibilities*. Grand Rapids: Eerdmans.

———. 1987. *Women and War*. New York: New York University Press.

———. 1981. *Public Man, Private Woman: Women in Social and Political Thought.* Princeton: Princeton University Press.

Elshtain, Jean Bethke, and J. Timothy Cloyd. 1996. *Politics and the Human Body: Assault on Dignity.* Nashville: Vanderbilt University Press.

Enloe, Cynthia. 2000. *Maneuvers: The International Politics of Militarizing Women's Lives.* Berkeley: University of California Press.

———. 1989. *Bananas, Beaches, and Bases: Making Feminist Sense of International Relations.* Berkeley: University of California Press.

———. 1983. *Does Khaki Become You? The Militarization of Women's Lives.* London: Pluto Press.

Epp, Roger. 1991. "The 'Augustinian Moment' in International Politics: Niebuhr, Butterfield, Wight and the Reclaiming of a Tradition." International Politics Research Paper, no. 10. Department of International Politics, University College of Wales, Aberystwyth.

Europol. 2009. *TE-SAT: EU Terrorism Situation and Trend Report.* The Hague: Europol. https://www.europol.europa.eu/sites/default/files/publications /tesat2009_0.pdf.

Executive Secretary on National Security. 1959. "National Security Council Report—68." http://www.trumanlibrary.org/whistlestop/study_collec tions/coldwar/documents/pdf/10-1.pdf.

Farah, Douglas. 2006. "The Strategic Challenge of Failed States." International Assessment and Strategy Center, 25 September. http://www.strategy center.net/research/pubID.120/pub_detail.asp.

Ferraro, Vincent. 1996. "Dependency Theory: An Introduction." In *The Development Economics Reader*, ed. Giorgio Secondi, 58–64. London: Routledge, 2008. https://www.mtholyoke.edu/acad/intrel/depend.htm.

Foreign Policy. 2010a. "FAQ & Methodology." http://www.foreignpolicy.com/ articles/2009/06/22/2009_failed_states_index_faq_methodology.

———. 2010b. "The Failed State Index 2009." *Foreign Policy*, 22 June. http:// www.foreignpolicy.com/articles/2009/06/22/the_2009_failed_states _index.

Fotion, Nicholas. 2007. *War and Ethics: A New Just War Theory.* New York: Continuum Books.

———. 2000. "Reactions to War: Pacifism, Realism, and Just War Theory." In *Ethics in International Affairs*, ed. Andrew Valls, 15–32. New York: Rowman and Littlefield.

Franzia-Roig, Manuel. 2009. "Politicians' Scandals Elevate the Profile of a Spiritual Haven on C Street SE." *Washington Post*, 26 June. http://www

.washingtonpost.com/wp-dyn/content/article/2009/06/25/AR200906
2504480.html.

Friedman, Uri. 2011. "A Brief History of Plan Colombia." *Foreign Policy*, 28
October. http://www.foreignpolicy.com/articles/2011/10/27/plan_colom
bia_a_brief_history#3.

Frost, Mervyn. 1996. *Ethics in International Relations*. Cambridge: Cambridge
University Press.

Fund for Peace. 2012. "Failed States Index." Washington, DC: The Fund for
Peace. http://www.fundforpeace.org/global/?q=fsi-grid2012.

———. 2010. "Failed States Index Score 2007." Washington, DC: The Fund
for Peace. http://www.fundforpeace.org/global/?q=fsi-grid2007.

Gaddis, John Lewis. 1987. *The Long Peace: Inquiries in the History of the Cold
War*. Cambridge: Cambridge University Press.

Galtung, Johan. 1969. "Violence, Peace, and Peace Research." *Journal of Peace
Research* 6 (3): 167–91.

Galtung, Johan, and Tord Höivik. 1971. "Structural and Direct Violence: A
Note on Operationalization." *Journal of Peace Research* 8 (1): 71–76.

Ganor, Boaz. 2005. *The Counter-Terrorism Puzzle: A Guide for Decision Makers*.
London: Transaction.

Gardinier, Suzanne. 1993. *The New World*. Pittsburgh: University of Pittsburgh Press.

Garfield, Richard. 2002. "Economic Sanctions, Humanitarianism, and Conflict After the Cold War." *Social Justice* 29 (3): 94–107.

Garnett, Richard W. 2006. "Campaigning from the Pulpit: Why Not?" *USA
Today*, 16 April. http://usatoday30.usatoday.com/news/opinion/editorials
/2006-04-16-forum-religion_x.htm.

Gentry, Caron E. 2014. "Epistemic Bias: Non-State Actors and Just War's
Legitimate Authority." In *The Future of Just War: New Critical Essays*, ed.
Caron E. Gentry and Amy E. Eckert. Forthcoming. Athens: University of
Georgia Press.

———. 2011. "The Neo-Orientalist Narrations of Women's Involvement
in Al Qaeda." In *Women, Gender, and Terrorism*, ed. Laura Sjoberg and
Caron E. Gentry, 176–93. Athens: University of Georgia Press.

———. 2009. "The Necessity of Popular Support: Locke, Al Qaeda, and the
War on Terror." In *Rethinking the 21st Century: "New" Problems, "Old"
Solutions*, ed. Amy Eckert and Laura Sjoberg, 22–45. London: Zed Books.

Gettlemen, Jeffrey. 2010. "Africa's Forever Wars: Why the Continent's Conflicts Never End." *Foreign Policy* (March/April). http://www.foreignpolicy
.com/articles/2010/02/22/africas_forever_wars?page=full.

Gordon, Ruth. 1997. "Saving Failed States: Sometimes a Neocolonialist Notion." *American University Journal of International Law* 12 (6): 904–74.

Gouws, Amanda. 2005. *(Un)thinking Citizenship*. Burlington: Ashgate.

Gray, Christopher M. 1999. "The Struggle for the Soul of American Foreign Policy." *Orbis* 43 (3): 497–597. http://go.galegroup.com/ps/i.do?id= GALE%7CA57785719&v=2.1&u=stand&it=r&p=EAIM&sw=w.

Greene, Graham. 2005. *The Power and the Glory*. London: Vintage Classics.

Grier, Peter. 2006. "Is War in Iraq a Shield against Attacks at Home?" *Christian Science Monitor*, 18 September. http://www.csmonitor.com/2006/0918 /p03s02-usfp.html.

Hampson, Daphne. 1990. *Theology and Feminism*. Oxford: Basil Blackwell.

Hauerwas, Stanley. 2001. *With the Grain of the Universe*. Grand Rapids: Brazos Press.

———. 1983. *The Peaceable Kingdom*. Notre Dame: University of Notre Dame Press.

———. 1981. *A Community of Character*. Notre Dame: University of Notre Dame Press.

Hauerwas, Stanley, John Berkmann, and Michael Cartwright, eds. 2001. *The Hauerwas Reader*. Durham: Duke University Press.

Hauerwas, Stanley, and Romand Coles. 2008. *Christianity, Democracy, and the Radical Ordinary: Conversations between a Radical Democrat and a Christian*. Eugene: Cascade Books.

Hauerwas, Stanley, and Jean Vanier. 2008. *Living Gently in a Violent World: The Prophetic Witness of Weakness*. Downer's Grove, IL: InterVarsity Press.

Hauerwas, Stanley, and Samuel Wells, eds. 2004. *The Blackwell Companion to Christian Ethics*. Malden: Blackwell.

Hearn, Jeff. 2004. "From Hegemonic Masculinity to the Hegemony of Men." *Feminist Theory* 5 (1): 49–72.

Heathershaw, John. 2008. "Unpacking the Liberal Peace: The Dividing and Merging of Peacebuilding Discourses." *Millennium: Journal of International Studies* 36 (3): 597–622.

Held, Virginia. 2011. *How Terrorism Is Wrong: Morality and Political Violence*. Oxford: Oxford University Press.

Herz, John H. 1950. "Idealist Internationalism and the Security Dilemma." *World Politics* 2 (2): 157–80.

al-Hibri, Azizah Y. 2001. "Women and the Taliban." *Philadelphia Inquirer*, 11 March. http://www.alhewar.com/women_and_the_taliban__azizah_al hibri.htm.

Hirschmann, Nancy J. 1992. *Rethinking Obligation: A Feminist Method for Political Theory*. Ithaca: Cornell University Press.

Hoffman, Bruce. 2006. *Inside Terrorism*. New York: Columbia University Press.

ICISS (International Commission on Intervention and State Sovereignty). 2001. *The Responsibility to Protect*. Ottawa: International Development Research Centre.

Ignatieff, Michael. 1998. *The Warrior's Honor*. New York: Macmillan.

———. 1993. *Blood and Belonging: Journeys into the New Nationalism*. New York: Noonday Press.

Iraq Body Count. 2011. London: Conflict Casualties Monitor. http://www.iraqbodycount.org/.

Jackson, Richard. 2005. *Writing the War on Terrorism*. Manchester: Manchester University Press.

Jackson, Timothy. 2003. *The Priority of Love: Christian Charity and Social Justice*. Princeton: Princeton University Press.

Johnson, James Turner. 2011. *Ethics and the Use of Force: Just War in Historical Perspective*. Burlington: Ashgate.

———. 2006. "Humanitarian Intervention after Iraq: Just War and International Law Perspectives." *Journal of Military Ethics* 5 (2): 114–27.

———. 2005. "Just War, As It Was and Is." *First Things* (January). http://www.firstthings.com/print/article/2007/01/just-waras-it-was-and-is-2?keep This=true&.

———. 1999. *Morality and Contemporary Warfare*. New Haven: Yale University Press.

———. 1981. *Just War Tradition and the Restraint of War*. Princeton: Princeton University Press.

Johnson, Stephen. 2001. "Helping Colombia Fix Its Plan to Curb Drug Trafficking, Violence, and Insurgency." Washington, DC: The Heritage Foundation, 26 April. http://www.heritage.org/research/reports/2001/04/helping-colombia-fix-its-plan?fb=true.

Kaldor, Mary. 2007. *Human Security*. London: Polity Press.

———. 1999. *New and Old Wars: Organized Violence in a Global Era*. London: Polity Press.

Kegley, Charles W. 2009. *World Politics: Trend and Transformation*. 12th ed. Boston: Cengage Learning.

Kegley, Charles W., and Eugene R. Wittkopf. 2003. *World Politics: Trend and Transformation*. 8th ed. Belmont: Wadsworth.

Kennan, George ("X"). 1947. "The Sources of Soviet Conduct." *Foreign Affairs*, 25–26 July, 566–82.

Kennedy-Pipe, Caroline. 2000. "From Cold Wars to New Wars." In *International Security in a Global Age*, ed. Clive Jones and Caroline Kennedy-Pipe, 9–27. London: Routledge.

King, Martin Luther. 1998. "Pilgrimage to Nonviolence." In *The Autobiography of Martin Luther King, Jr.*, ed. Clayborne Carson. New York: Warner Books. http://mlk-kpp01.stanford.edu/index.php/kingpapers/article/chapter_13_pilgrimage_to_nonviolence/.

Lake, David A. 1992. "Powerful Pacifists: Democratic States and War." *American Political Science Review* 86 (1): 24–37.

Langan, John. 1991. "The Elements of St. Augustine's Just War Theory." In *The Ethics of St. Augustine*, ed. William S. Babcock, 169–90. Atlanta: Scholars Press.

Lango, John W. 2006. "Last Resort and Coercive Threats: Relating a Just War Principle to a Military Practice." http://isme.tamu.edu/JSCOPE06/Lango06.pdf.

Lederach, John Paul. 2010. "From Conflict Resolution to Conflict Transformation to Strategic Peacebuilding." Lecture given at the Teaching Peace in the 21st Century Summer Institute for Faculty, Kroc Institute, University of Notre Dame, 15 June.

———. 1995. *Preparing for Peace: Conflict Transformation Across Cultures.* Syracuse: Syracuse University Press.

Levinas, Emmanuel. 2006. *Humanism of the Other*. Introduction by Richard A. Cohen. Trans. Nidra Poller. Urbana: University of Illinois Press.

Levy, Donald P. 2009. "Hegemonic Masculinity." Blackwell Reference Online. http://www.blackwellreference.com/public/tocnode?id=g97814051243 31_chunk_g978140512433114_ss1–22.

Logan, Justin, and Christopher Preble. 2006. "Failed States and Flawed Logic: The Case against a Standing Nation-Building Office." *Policy Analysis*, no. 560, 11 January. http://www.cato.org/publications/policy-analysis/failed-states-flawed-logic-case-against-standing-nationbuilding-office.

Lopez, George. 2010. "The History and Contested Areas of Peace Studies." Lecture given at the Teaching Peace in the 21st Century Summer Institute for Faculty, Kroc Institute, University of Notre Dame, 14 June.

Lopez, George, and David Cortright. 2004. "Containing Iraq: Sanctions Worked." *Foreign Affairs* (July/August). http://s06.middlebury.edu/ECON 0340A/Containing%20Iraq.pdf.

Lovin, Robin W. 2008. *Christian Realism and the New Realities*. Cambridge: Cambridge University Press.

———. 2007. "Christian Realism and the Successful Modern State." *Studies in Christian Ethics* 20 (1): 55–67.

———. 1995. *Reinhold Niebuhr and Christian Realism.* Cambridge: Cambridge University Press.

MacKinnon, Catharine A. 2001. *Sex Equality.* New York: Foundation Press.

Mallaby, Sebastian. 2002. "The Reluctant Imperialist: Terrorist, Failed States, and the Case for American Empire." *Foreign Affairs* (March/April): 2–7.

Marcella, Gabriel. 2009. *Democratic Governance and the Rule of Law: Lessons from Colombia.* New York: Strategic Studies Institute.

———. 2003. *The United States and Colombia: The Journey from Ambiguity to Strategic Clarity.* New York: Strategic Studies Institute.

May, Larry. 2007. *War Crimes and Just War.* Cambridge: Cambridge University Press.

McCarthy, Stephen. 2004. "The Buddhist Political Rhetoric of Aung San Suu Kyi." *Contemporary Buddhism* 5 (2): 67–81.

Mertus, Julie. 2000. *War's Offensive on Women: The Humanitarian Challenge in Bosnia, Kosovo, and Afghanistan.* West Hartford: Kumarian Press.

Miller, Jean Baker. 1986. *Toward a New Psychology of Women.* Boston: Beacon Press.

Moghadam, Valentine M. 2003. *Modernizing Women: Gender and Social Change in the Middle East.* 2nd ed. Boulder: Lynne Rienner.

Moltmann, Jürgen. 1974. *The Crucified God: The Cross of Christ as the Foundation and Criticism of Christian Theology.* New York: Harper & Row.

Morgenthau, Hans. 1978. *Politics among Nations: The Struggle for Power and Peace.* New York: Alfred A. Knopf.

Moser, Caroline, and Fiona C. Clark, eds. 2001. *Victims, Perpetrators, or Actors? Gender, Armed Conflict, and Political Violence.* London: Zed Books.

Moyers, Bill. 2008. "Bill Moyers Interviews Andrew Bacevich." *Bill Moyers Journal,* 15 August. http://www.pbs.org/moyers/journal/08152008/profile.html.

Moyo, Dambiso. 2009. *Dead Aid: Why Aid Is Not Working and How There Is Another Way for Africa.* London: Penguin UK.

Naylor, R. T. 2001. *Economic Warfare: Sanctions, Embargo Busting, and Their Human Cost.* Boston: Northeastern University Press.

Newman, Elizabeth. 2007. "Untamed Hospitality." *Christian Reflection: A Series in Faith and Ethics* 25: 11–19. Waco: Center for Christian Ethics, Baylor University.

Newsweek. 2009. "Best. Books. Ever." *Newsweek* 154 (1/2), 13 July, 56.

Niebuhr, H. Richard. 1956. *The Purpose of the Church and Its Ministry: Reflection on the Aims of Theological Education.* New York: Harper.

———. 1932. "The Grace of Doing Nothing." *Christian Century*, 23 March, 378–80.

Niebuhr, Reinhold. 2008. *The Irony of American History.* Chicago: University of Chicago Press.

———. 1986. "Why the Christian Church Is Not Pacifist." In *The Essential Reinhold Niebuhr*, ed. Robert McAfee Brown, 102–22. New Haven: Yale University Press.

———. 1964. *The Nature and Destiny of Man: A Christian Interpretation.* Vol. 1. New York: Charles Scribner's Sons.

———. 1962a. "American Hegemony and the Prospects for Peace." *Annals of the American Academy of Political and Social Sciences* 342 (July): 154–60.

———. 1962b. "History as Seen from the Radical Right." *New Leader* 45, 16 April, 24.

———. 1961. "Living with Fear." *New Leader* 44, 13 November, 23.

———. 1957. "Theology and Political Thought in the Western World." *The Ecumenical Review* 9 (3): 253–62.

———. 1956. *An Interpretation of Christian Ethics.* Cleveland: Meridian Books.

———. 1932a. *Moral Man and Immoral Society.* New York: Charles Scribner's Sons.

———. 1932b. "Must We Do Nothing?" *Christian Century* 30 (March): 415–17.

Niebuhr, Reinhold, and Alan Heimert. 1963. *A Nation So Conceived.* New York: Charles Scribner's Sons.

Nossal, Kim Richard. 1989. "International Sanctions as International Punishment." *International Organization* 43 (2): 301–22.

NPR (National Public Radio). 2009. "'Family': Fundamentalism, Friends in High Places." *Fresh Air*, National Public Radio, 1 July. http://www.npr.org/templates/story/story.php?storyId=106115324.

NuclearFiles.org. 1998. "Economic Aspects of Conversion." Santa Barbara: Nuclear Age Peace Foundation. http://www.nuclearfiles.org/menu/key-issues/ethics/issues/military/economic-aspects-conversion.htm.

O'Brien, William V. 1992. "Just-War Doctrine in a Nuclear Context." In *War in the Twentieth Century: Sources in Theological Ethics*, ed. Richard B. Miller, 311–46. Louisville: Westminster/John Knox Press.

O'Driscoll, Cian. 2007. "Jean Bethke Elshtain's Just War against Terror: A Tale of Two Cities." *International Relations* 21 (4): 485–92.

Ottaway, Marina, and Stefan Mair. 2004. "States at Risk and Failed States: Putting Security First." *Policy Outlook* (September). http://www.policy archive.org/handle/10207/bitstreams/6593.pdf.

Patterson, Eric. 2003a. "Niebuhr and His Contemporaries: Introduction to Christian Realism." In *Reinhold Niebuhr and His Critics: Reassessing the Contributions of Niebuhr and His Contemporaries*, ed. Eric Patterson, 1–24. Lanham: University Press of America.

———. 2003b. "Niebuhr and His Critics: Realistic Optimism in World Politics." In *Reinhold Niebuhr and His Critics: Reassessing the Contributions of Niebuhr and His Contemporaries*, ed. Eric Patterson, 25–51. Lanham: University Press of America.

Patton, Paul. 2003. "Concepts and Politics in Derrida and Deleuze." *Critical Horizons* 4 (2): 157–75.

Peperzak, Adriaan. 1993. *To the Other: An Introduction to the Philosophy of Emmanuel Levinas*. West Lafayette: Purdue University Press.

Person, Ethel Spector. 1978. "Review: *Toward a New Psychology of Women* by Jean Baker Miller; *Psychic War in Men and Women* by Helen Block Lewis; *The Mermaid and the Minotaur: Sexual Arrangements and Human Malaise* by Dorothy Dinnerstein." *Signs* 4 (1): 163–67.

Peterson, V. Spike. 1999. "Sexing Political Identities/Nationalism as Heterosexism." *International Feminist Journal of Politics* 1 (1): 34–65.

Peterson, V. Spike, and Anne Sisson Runyan. 2010. *Global Gender Issues in the New Millennium*. Boulder: Westview Press.

Pew Forum. 2010. "Tolerance and Tension: Islam and Christianity in Sub-Saharan Africa." Pew Forum on Religion and Public Life, 15 April. http:// pewforum.org/docs/?DocID=515.

———. 2009a. "The Torture Debate: A Closer Look." Pew Forum on Religion and Public Life, 7 May. http://pewforum.org/docs/?DocID=417.

———. 2009b. "The Religious Dimensions of the Torture Debate." Pew Forum on Religion and Public Life, 7 May. http://pewforum.org/docs /?DocID=156.

Plan Colombia. 1999. Washington, DC: The United States Institute for Peace.

Poe, Danielle. 2008. "Replacing Just War Theory with an Ethics of Sexual Difference." *Hypatia* 23 (2): 33–47.

Pohl, Christine D. 2007. "Building a Place for Hospitality." *Christian Reflection: A Series in Faith and Ethics* 25: 27–36. Waco: Center for Christian Ethics, Baylor University.

Pottebaum, David. 2005. *Conflict, Poverty, Inequality, and Economic Growth*. USAID. http://pdf.usaid.gov/pdf_docs/PNADK690.pdf.

Power, Paul F. 1963. "Toward a Re-Evaluation of Gandhi's Political Thought." *Western Political Quarterly* 16 (1): 98–108.

Power, Samantha. 2002. "Genocide and America." *New York Review of Books*, 14 March, 15–18.

Ramsey, Paul. 2002. *The Just War: Force and Political Responsibility*. Lanham: Rowman and Littlefield.

———. 1992. "The Just War According to Saint Augustine." In *Just War Theory*, ed. Jean Bethke Elshtain, 8–22. New York: New York University Press.

———. 1954. *Basic Christian Ethics*. New York: Charles Scribner's Sons.

Rengger, Nicholas. 2012. Personal communication, St. Andrews, Scotland, 24 July.

———. 2004. "Review: Just a War Against Terror? Jean Bethke Elshtain's Burden and American Power." *International Affairs* 80 (1): 107–16.

———. 2002. "On the Just War Tradition in the Twenty-First Century." *International Affairs* 78 (3): 353–63.

Reus-Smit, Christian. 1999. *The Moral Purpose of the State: Culture, Social Identity, and Institutional Rationality in International Relations*. Princeton: Princeton University Press.

Reychler, Luc. 2006. "Challenges of Peace Research." *International Journal of Peace Studies* 11 (1): 1–16. http://www.gmu.edu/programs/icar/ijps/vol11 _1/11n1Reychler.pdf.

Rich, Adrienne. 1993. *What Is Found There: Notebooks on Poetry and Politics*. New York: W. W. Norton.

Richmond, Oliver P. 2008. *Peace in International Relations: A New Agenda*. London: Routledge.

———. 2002. *Maintaining Order, Making Peace*. Houndmills, Basingstoke: Palgrave Macmillan.

Rissman, B. 2004. "Gender as a Social Structure: Theory Wrestling with Activism." *Gender and Society* 18 (4): 429–50.

Rogers, Eugene F., Jr. 2005. *After the Spirit: A Constructive Pneumatology from Resources Outside the Modern West*. Grand Rapids: Eerdmans.

Rotberg, Robert I. 2010. "Disorder in the Ranks: A Different Take on What Makes a 'Failed' State." *Foreign Policy*, 22 June. http://www.foreignpolicy .com/articles/2009/06/22/2009_failed_states_index_disorder_in_the _ranks.

———. 2002. "Failed States in a World of Terror." *Foreign Affairs* 81 (4): 127–40.

Royden, Alexa. 2014. "An Alternative to Nuclear Weapons? Proportionality, Discrimination and the Conventional Global Strike Program." In *The*

Future of Just War: New Critical Essays, ed. Caron E. Gentry and Amy E. Eckert. Forthcoming. Athens: University of Georgia Press.

Ruddick, Sara. 1989. *Maternal Thinking: Toward a Politics of Peace*. Boston: Beacon Press.

Ryan, Stephen. 2003. "Peace and Conflict Studies Today." *Global Review of Ethnopolitics* 2 (2): 75–82.

Sachs, Jeffrey. 2008. *Common Wealth: Economics for a Crowded Planet*. New York: Penguin Press.

———. 2007. "No Development, No Peace." *Beijing Review*, 16 August, 16.

———. 2005. *The End of Poverty: Economic Possibilities for Our Time*. New York: Penguin Press.

Sagan, Scott, and Kenneth Waltz. 1995. *The Spread of Nuclear Weapons: A Debate*. New York: W. W. Norton.

Said, Edward. 2004. "Orientalism." In *A Critical and Cultural Theory Reader*, ed. Anthony Easthope and Kate McGowan, 55–61. Toronto: University of Toronto Press.

———. 1985. "Orientalism Reconsidered." *Cultural Critique* 1: 89–107.

———. 1978. *Orientalism*. New York: Penguin Press.

Seliger, Martin. 1963. "Locke's Theory of Revolutionary Action." *Western Political Quarterly* 16 (3): 548–68.

Shinn, Roger L. 2003. "Christian Realism in a Pluralistic Society: Interactions between Niebuhr and Morgenthau, Kennan, and Schlesinger." In *Reinhold Niebuhr and His Critics: Reassessing the Contributions of Niebuhr and His Contemporaries*, ed. Eric Patterson, 177–98. Lanham: University Press of America.

Singer, P. W. 2009. "Military Robots and the Laws of War." *New Atlantis* (winter). http://www.thenewatlantis.com/publications/military-robots -and-the-laws-of-war.

Sjoberg, Laura. 2006. *Gender, Justice, and the Wars in Iraq: A Feminist Reformulation of Just War Theory*. Lanham: Lexington Books.

Sjoberg, Laura, and Caron E. Gentry. 2007. *Mothers, Monsters, Whores: Women's Violence in Global Politics*. London: Zed Books.

Snider, Don, and Chris Hickey. 2003. "Christian Citizenship and American Empire." *Brandywine Review of Faith and International Affairs* (fall): 3–11.

Spivak, Gayatri Chakravorty. 1998. "Can the Subaltern Speak?" In *Marxism and the Interpretation of Culture*, ed. Cary Nelson and Lawrence Grossberg, 24–28. London: Macmillan.

Stassen, Glen H. 2006. "Just Peacemaking Theory for International Cooperation in Preventing Terrorism." *Carson Newman Studies* 11 (1): 150–62.

————. 2005. "The Ethics of War and Peacemaking." In *Toward an Evangelical Public Policy: Political Strategies for the Health of the Nation*, ed. Ronald J. Sider and Dianne Knipper, 284–306. Grand Rapids: Baker Books.

State Failure Task Force. 2000. *State Failure Task Force: Phase III Findings*. College Park: Center for International Development and Conflict Management, University of Maryland. http://www.cidcm.umd.edu/publications /papers/SFTF%20Phase%20III%20Report%20Final.pdf.

Steans, Jill. 2006. *Gender and International Relations: Issues, Debates and Future Directions*. London: Polity Press.

Stephen, Maria, and Erica Chenoweth. 2008. "Why Civil Resistance Works: The Strategic Logic of Nonviolent Conflict." *International Security* 33 (1): 7–44.

Stone, Carolyn. 1996. "Gender Values and Identity: Carol Gilligan's Work on Women's Moral Development." In *Women, Power and Resistance: An Introduction to Women's Studies*, ed. Tess Cosslet, Alison Easton, and Penny Summerfield, 165–75. Buckingham: Open University Press.

Stout, Jeffrey. 2005. *Democracy and Tradition*. Princeton: New Forum Books.

Strange, Susan. 1988. *States and Markets*. New York: Continuum.

Swinburne, Richard. 1994. *The Christian God*. Oxford: Oxford University Press.

Sylvester, Christine. 2002. *Feminist International Relations: An Unfinished Journey*. Cambridge: Cambridge University Press.

————. 1999. *Feminist Theory and International Relations in a Postmodern Era*. Cambridge: Cambridge University Press.

————. 1990. *Feminists and Realists on Autonomy and Obligation in International Relations*. University of Southern California, Center for International Studies, Los Angeles.

Thompson, Dennis L. 1975. "The Basic Doctrines and Concepts of Reinhold Niebuhr's Political Thought." *Journal of Church and State* 17: 275–99.

Thucydides. 2009. "The Melian Dialogue." In *History of the Peloponnesian War*. http://www.mtholyoke.edu/acad/intrel/melian.htm.

Tickner, J. Ann. 2001. *Gendering World Politics*. New York: Columbia University Press.

————. 1992. *Gender in International Relations: Feminist Perspectives on Achieving Global Security*. New York: Columbia University Press.

Toulmin, Stephen. 1990. *Cosmopolis: Hidden Agenda of Modernity*. Chicago: University of Chicago Press.

Ulrich, Andrew. 2006. "Balance Democracy with Power: Responsibility, Order, and Justice in Reinhold Niebuhr's World View, 1940–1949." Paper given at the James A. Rawley Graduate Conference in the Humanities, Lincoln, NE, 8 April. http://digitalcommons.unl.edu/historyrawleyconference/3.

United Nations General Assembly. 2005. *In Larger Freedom: Towards Development, Security, and Human Rights for All.* Report of the Secretary General, United Nations, New York. http://daccess-dds-ny.un.org/doc/UNDOC /GEN/N05/270/78/PDF/N0527078.pdf?OpenElement.

U.S. Catholics Bishops. 1983. "Pastoral Letter on War and Peace." Nuclearfiles. org. http://www.nuclearfiles.org/menu/key-issues/ethics/issues/religious /us-catholic-bishops-pastoral-letter.htm.

Veillette, Connie. 2005. "Plan Colombia: A Progress Report." CRS Report for Congress. Washington, DC: Congressional Research Service, Library of Congress. http://www.fas.org/sgp/crs/row/RL32774.pdf.

Volf, Miroslav. 2008. "Are We Safe Yet?" Welcoming remarks given at the Sarah Smith Memorial Conference, Yale Divinity School, New Haven. http:// www.yale.edu/faith/downloads/Sarah_Smith_Conf_Welcome_2008 _Miroslav_Volf.pdf.

———. 1997. "Exclusion and Embrace: Theological Reflection in the Wake of 'Ethnic Cleansing.'" In *A Spacious Heart: Essays on Identity and Belonging*, ed. Judith Gundry-Volf and Miroslav Volf, 33–50. Harrisburg: Trinity Press International.

———. 1996. *Exclusion and Embrace.* Nashville: Abingdon Press.

Walker, William. 2000. "Nuclear Order and Disorder." *International Affairs* 76 (4): 703–24.

Wallerstein, Immanuel. 1974. *The Modern World System.* Vol. 1. London: Academic Press.

Waltz, Kenneth. 1979. *Theory of International Politics.* New York: McGraw-Hill.

———. 1959. *Man, the State, and War.* New York: Columbia University Press.

Walzer, Michael. 1977. *Just and Unjust Wars.* New York: Basic Books.

Ward, Michael T. 2006. "The Case for International Trusteeship in Haiti." *Canadian Military Journal* (autumn): 25–34.

Webb, Michael, and Stephen Krasner. 1989. "Hegemonic Stability Theory: An Empirical Assessment." *Review of International Studies* 15 (2): 183–98.

Wendt, Alexander. 1992. "Anarchy Is What States Make of It: The Social Construction of Power Politics." *International Organization* 46 (2): 391–425.

Wester, Eric. 2007. "Last Resort and Preemption: Using Armed Force as a Moral and Penultimate Choice." *Parameters* (summer): 59–70.

Williams, Michael C. 2011. "Securitization and the Liberalism of Fear." *Security Dialogue* 42 (4–5): 453–63.

————. 2003. "Words, Images, Enemies: Securitization and International Politics." *International Studies Quarterly* 47: 511–31.

Williams, Robert E. 1986. "Christian Realism and 'the Bomb': Reinhold Niebuhr and the Dilemmas of the Nuclear Age." *Journal of Church and State* 28 (2): 289–304.

Wright, Lawrence. 2006. *The Looming Tower: Al-Qaeda and the Road to 9/11.* New York: Vintage Books.

Wright, N. T. 1994. *Following Jesus: Biblical Reflections on Discipleship.* Grand Rapids: Eerdmans.

Yoder, John Howard. 1978. *The Politics of Jesus.* Grand Rapids: Eerdmans.

Yuval-Davis, Nira. 1997. *Gender and Nation.* Thousand Oaks, CA: Sage.

Zarkov, Dubravka. 1995. "Gender, Orientalism and the History of Ethnic Hatred in the Former Yugoslavia." *Crossfires: Nationalism, Racism and Gender in Europe*, ed. Phoenix Lutz and Yuval-Davis, 105–21. London: Pluto Press.

Zaw, Susan Khin. 1992. "Morality and Survival in the Nuclear Age." In *Just War Theory*, ed. Jean Bethke Elshtain, 234–59. New York: New York University Press.

Index

CARON E. GENTRY

is lecturer in the School of International Relations

at the University of St. Andrews.

She is coauthor with Laura Sjoberg of

Mothers, Monsters, and Whores: Women's Violence in Global Politics.